Pélléas and Mélisande

Maurice Maeterlinck

PÉLLÉAS AND MÉLISANDE

CONTENTS

PRÉFACE.

On m'a demande plus d'une fois si mes drames, de *La Princesse Maleine* à *La Mort de Tintagiles*, avaient été réellement écrits pour un théâtre de marionettes, ainsi que je l'avais affirmé dans l'edition originale de cette sauvage petite légende des malheurs de Maleine. En vérité, ils ne furent pas écrits pour des acteurs ordinaires. Il n'y avait là nul désir ironique et pas la moindre humilité non plus. Je croyais sincèrement et je crois encore aujourd'hui, que les poèmes meurent lorsque des êtres vivants s'y introduisent. Un jour, dans un écrit dont je ne retrouve plus que quelques fragments mutilés, j'ai essayé d'expliquer ces choses qui dorment, sans doute, au fond de notre instinct et qu'il est bien difficile de reveiller complètement. J'y constatais d'abord, qu'une inquiètude nous attendait à tout spectacle auquel nous assistions et qu'une déception à peu près ineffable accompagnait toujours la chute du rideau. N'est-il pas évident que le Macbeth ou l'Hamlet que nous voyons sur la scène ne ressemble pas au Macbeth ou à l'Hamlet du livre? Qu'il a visiblement retrogradé dans le sublime? Qu'une grande partie des efforts du poète qui voulait créer avant tout une vie supérieure, une vie plus proche de notre âme, a été annulée par une force ennemie qui ne peut se manifester qu'en ramenant cette vie supérieure au niveau de la vie ordinaire? Il y a peut-être, me disais-je, aux sources de ce malaise, un très ancien malentendu, à la suite duquel le théâtre ne fut jamais exactement ce qu'il est dans l'instinct de la foule, à savoir: *le temple du Rêve*. Il faut admettre, ajoutai-je, que le théâtre, du moins en ses tendances, est un art. Mais je n'y trouve pas la marque des autres arts. L'art use toujours d'un détour et n'agit pas directement. Il a pour mission suprême la révélation de i'infini et de la grandeur ainsi que la beauté secrète, de l'homme. Mais montrer au doigt à l'enfant qui nous accompagne, les étoiles d'une unit de Juillet, ce n'est pas faire une oeuvre d'art. Il faut que l'art agisse comme les abeilles. Elles n'apportent pas aux larves de la ruche les fleurs des champs qui renferment leur avenir et leur vie. Les larves mourraient sous ces fleurs sans se douter de rien. Il faut que les abeilles nourricières apportent à ces nymphes aveugles l'âme même de ces fleurs, et c'est alors seulement qu'elles trouveront sans le savoir en ce miel mystérieux la substance des ailes qui un jour les emporteront à leur tour dans l'espace. Or, le poème était une oeuvre d'art et portait ces obliques et admirables marques. Mais la représentation vient le contredire. Elle chasse vraiment les cygnes du grand lac, et elle rejette les perles dans l'abîme. Elle remet les choses exactement au point où elles étaient avant la venue du poète. La densité mystique de l'oeuvre d'art a disparue. Elle verse dans la même erreur que celui qui après avoir vanté à ses auditeurs l'admirable *Annonciation* de Vinci, par exemple, s'imaginerait qu'il a fait pénétrer dans leurs âmes la beauté surnaturelle de cette peinture en reproduisant, en un tableau vivant, tous les détails du grand chef-d'oeuvre florentin.

Qui sait si ce n'est pas pour ces raisons cachées que l'on est obligé de s'avouer que la plupart des grands poèmes de l'humanité ne sont pas scéniques? *Lear, Hamlet, Othello, Macbeth, Antoine et Cléopâtre*, ne peuvent être représentés, et il est dangereux de les voir sur la scène. Quelque chose d'Hamlet est mort pour nous du jour où nous l'avons vu mourir sous nos yeux. Le spectre d'un acteur l'a détrôné, et nous ne pouvons plus écarter l'usurpateur de nos rêves. Ouvrez les portes, ouvrez le livre, le prince antérieur ne revient plus. Il a perdu la faculté de vivre selon la beauté la plus secrète de notre âme. Parfois son ombre passe encore en tremblant sur le seuil, mais désormais il n'ose plus, il ne peut plus entrer; et bien des voix sont mortes qui l'acclamaient en nous.

Je me souviens de cette mort de l'Hamlet de mes rêves. Un soir j'ouvris la porte à l'usurpateur du poème. L'acteur était illustre. Il entra. Un seul de ses regards me montra qu'il n'était pas Hamlet. Il ne le fut pas un seul instant pour moi. Je le vis s'agiter durant trois heures dans le mensonge. Je voyais clairement qu'il avait ses propres destinées; et celles qu'il voulait représenter m'étaient indiciblement indifférentes à côté des siennes. Je voyais sa santé et ses habitudes, ses passions et ses tristesses, ses pensées et ses oeuvres, et il essayait vainement de m'intéresser à une vie qui n'était pas la sienne et que sa seule présence avait rendue factice. Depuis je le revois lorsque j'ouvre le livre et Elsinore n'est plus le palais d'autrefois . . .

"La vérité," dit quelque part Charles Lamb, "la vérité est que les caractères de Shakespeare sont tellement des objets de méditation plutôt que d'intérêt ou de curiosité relativement à leurs actes, que, tandis que nous lisons l'un de ses grands caractères criminels,—Macbeth, Richard, Iago même,—nous ne songeons pas tant aux crimes qu'ils commettent, qu'à l'ambition, à l'esprit d'aspiration, à l'activité intellectuelle qui les poussent à franchir ces barrières morales. Les actions nous affectent si peu, que, tandis que les impulsions, l'esprit intérieur en toute sa perverse grandeur, paraissent seuls réels et appellent seuls l'attention, le crime n'est comparativement rien. Mais lorsque nous voyons représenter ces choses, les actes sont comparativement tout, et les mobiles ne sont plus rien. L'émotion sublime où nous sommes entraînés par ces images de nuit et d'horreur qu'exprime Macbeth; ce solennel prélude où il s'oublie jusqu'à ce que l'horloge sonne l'heure qui doit l'appeler au meurtre de Duncan; lorsque nous ne lisons plus cela dans un livre, lorsque nous avons abandonné ce poste avantageux de l'abstraction d'où la lecture domine la vision, et lorsque nous voyons sous nos yeux, un homme en sa forme corporelle se préparer actuellement au meurtre; si le jeu de l'acteur est vrai et puissant, la pénible anxiété au sujet de l'acte, le naturel désir de le prévenir tout qu'il ne semble pas accompli, la trop puissante apparence de réalité, provoquent un malaise et une inquiétude qui détruisent totalement le plaisir que les mots apportent dans le livre, où l'acte ne nous oppresse jamais de la pénible sensation de sa présence, et semble plutôt appartenir à l'histoire; à quelque chose de passé et d'inévitable."

Charles Lamb a raison, et pour mille raisons bien plus profondes encore que celles qu'il nous donne. Le théâtre est le lien où meurent la plupart des chefs-d'oeuvre, parce que la représentation d'un chef-d'oeuvre à l'aide d'éléments accidentels et humains est antinomique. Tout chef-d'oeuvre est un symbole, et le symbole ne supporte pas la présence active de l'homme. Il suffit que le coq chante, dit Hamlet, pour que les spectres de la nuit s'évanouissent. Et de même, le poème perd sa vie "de la seconde sphère" lorsqu'un être de la sphère inférieure s'y introduit. L'accident ramène le symbole à l'accident; et le chef-d'oeuvre, en son essence, est mort durant le temps de cette présence et de ses traces.

Les Grecs n'ignorèrent pas cette antinomie, et leurs masques que nous ne comprenons plus ne servaient probablement qu'à atténuer la présence de l'homme et à soulager le symbole. Aux époques où le théâtre eut une vie véritable, il la dût peut-être uniquement à quelque circonstance ou à quelque artifice qui venait en aide du poème dans sa lutte contre l'homme. Ainsi, sous Elisabeth, par exemple, la déclamation était une sorte de mélopée, le jeu était conventionnel, et la scène aussi. Il en était à peu près de même sous Louis XIV. Le poème se retire à mesure que l'homme s'avance. Le poème veut nous arracher du pouvoir de nos sens et faire prédominer le passé et l'avenir; l'homme, au contraire, n'agit que sur nos sens et n'existe que pour autant qu'il puisse effacer cette prédomination. S'il entre en scène avec toutes ses puissances, et libre comme s'il entrait dans une forêt; si sa voix, ses gestes, et son attitude ne sont pas voilées par un grand nombre de conventions synthétiques; si l'on aperçoit un seul instant l'être vivant qu'il est et l'âme qu'il possède,—il n'y a pas de poème au monde qui ne recule devant lui. A ce moment précis, le spectacle du poème s'interrompt et nous assistons à une scène de la vie extérieure, qui, de même qu'une scène de la rue, de la rivière, ou du champ de bataille, a ses beautés éternelles et secrètes, mais qui est néanmoins impuissante à nous arracher du présent, parce qu'en cet instant nous n'avons pas la qualité pour apercevoir ces beautés invisibles, qui ne sont que "des fleurs offertes aux vers aveugles."

Et c'est pour ces raisons, et pour d'autres encore qu'on pourrait rechercher dans les mêmes parages, que j'avais destiné mes petits drames à des êtres indulgents aux poèmes, et que, faute de mieux, j'appelle "Marionettes."

MAURICE MAETERLINCK.

PÉLLÉAS AND MÉLISANDE

To Octave Mirbeau.

In witness of deep friendship, admiration, and gratitude.

M.M.

PERSONS

ARKËL, *King of Allemonde.*

GENEVIÈVE, *mother of Pélléas and Golaud.*

PÉLLÉAS, }
              } *grandsons of Arkël.*
GOLAUD, }

MÉLISANDE.

LITTLE YNIOLD, *son of Golaud (by a former marriage).*

A PHYSICIAN.

THE PORTER.

Servants, Beggars, etc.

ACT FIRST.

SCENE I.—*The gate of the castle.*

MAIDSERVANTS (*within*).
> Open the gate! Open the gate!

PORTER (*within*).
> Who is there? Why do you come and wake me up? Go out by the little gates; there are enough of them! . . .

A MAIDSERVANT (*within*).
> We have come to wash the threshold, the gate, and the steps; open, then! open!

ANOTHER MAIDSERVANT (*within*).
> There are going to be great happenings!

THIRD MAIDSERVANT (*within*).
> There are going to be great fêtes! Open quickly! . . .

THE MAIDSERVANTS.
> Open! open!

PORTER.
> Wait! wait! I do not know whether I shall be able to open it; . . . it is never opened . . . Wait till it is light . . .

FIRST MAIDSERVANT.
> It is light enough without; I see the sunlight through the chinks . . .

PORTER.

Here are the great keys . . . Oh! oh! how the bolts and the locks grate! . . . Help me! help me! . . .

MAIDSERVANTS.

We are pulling; we are pulling . . .

SECOND MAIDSERVANT.

It will not open . . .

FIRST MAIDSERVANT.

Ah! ah! It is opening! it is opening slowly!

PORTER.

How it shrieks! how it shrieks! it will wake up everybody . . .

SECOND MAIDSERVANT.

[*Appearing on the threshold.*] Oh, how light it is already out-of-doors!

FIRST MAIDSERVANT.

The sun is rising on the sea!

PORTER.

It is open . . . It is wide open! . . . [All the maidservants appear on the threshold and pass over it.]

FIRST MAIDSERVANT.

I am going to wash the sill first . . .

SECOND MAIDSERVANT.

We shall never be able to clean all this.

OTHER MAIDSERVANTS.

Fetch the water! fetch the water!

PORTER.

Yes, yes; pour on water; pour on water; pour on all the water of the Flood! You will never come to the end of it . . .

SCENE II.—A forest. MÉLISANDE discovered at the brink of a spring.

Enter GOLAUD.

GOLAUD.

I shall never be able to get out of this forest again.—God knows where that beast has led me. And yet I thought I had wounded him to death; and here are traces of blood. But now I have lost sight of him; I believe I am lost myself—my dogs can no longer find me—I shall retrace my steps . . .—I hear weeping . . . Oh! oh! what is there yonder by the water's edge? . . . A little girl weeping by the water's edge? [*He coughs.*]—She does not hear me. I cannot see her face. [*He approaches and touches MÉLISANDE on the shoulder.*] Why weepest thou? [*MÉLISANDE trembles, starts up, and would flee.*]—Do not be afraid. You have nothing to fear. Why are you weeping here all alone?

MÉLISANDE.

Do not touch me! do not touch me!

GOLAUD.

Do not be afraid . . . I will not do you any . . . Oh, you are beautiful!

MÉLISANDE.

Do not touch me! do not touch me! or I throw myself in the water! . . .

GOLAUD.

I will not touch you . . . See, I will stay here, against the tree. Do not be afraid. Has any one hurt you?

MÉLISANDE

Oh! yes! yes! yes! . . . *[She sobs profoundly.]*

GOLAUD.

Who has hurt you?

MÉLISANDE.

Every one! every one!

GOLAUD. What hurt have they done you?

MÉLISANDE.

I will not tell! I cannot tell! . . .

GOLAUD.

Come; do not weep so. Whence come you?

MÉLISANDE.

I have fled! . . . fled . . . fled . . .

GOLAUD.

Yes; but whence have you fled?

MÉLISANDE.

I am lost! . . . lost! . . . Oh! oh! lost here . . . I am not of this place . . . I was not born there . . .

GOLAUD.

Whence are you? Where were you born?

MÉLISANDE.

Oh! oh! far away from here! . . . far away . . . far away . . .

GOLAUD.

What is it shining so at the bottom of the water?

MÉLISANDE.

Where?—Ah! it is the crown he gave me. It fell as I was weeping . . .

GOLAUD.

A crown?—Who was it gave you a crown?—I will try to get it . . .

MÉLISANDE.

No, no; I will have no more of it! I will have no more of it! . . . I had rather die . . . die at once . . .

GOLAUD.

I could easily pull it out. The water is not very deep.

MÉLISANDE.

I will have no more of it! If you take it out, I throw myself in its place! . . .

GOLAUD.

No, no; I will leave it there. It could be reached without difficulty, nevertheless. It seems very beautiful.—Is it long since you fled?

MÉLISANDE.

Yes, yes! . . . Who are you?

GOLAUD.

I am Prince Golaud,—grandson of Arkël, the old King of Allemonde . . .

MÉLISANDE.

Oh, you have gray hairs already . . .

GOLAUD.

Yes; some, here, by the temples . . .

MÉLISANDE

And in your beard, too . . . Why do you look at me so?

GOLAUD.

I am looking at your eyes.—Do you never shut your eyes?

MÉLISANDE.

Oh, yes; I shut them at night . . .

GOLAUD.

Why do you look so astonished?

MÉLISANDE.

You are a giant?

GOLAUD.

I am a man like the rest . . .

MÉLISANDE.

Why have you come here?

GOLAUD.

I do not know, myself. I was hunting in the forest, I was chasing a wild boar. I mistook the road.—You look very young. How old are you?

MÉLISANDE.

I am beginning to be cold . . .

GOLAUD.

Will you come with me!

MÉLISANDE.

No, no; I will stay here . . .

GOLAUD.

You cannot stay here all alone. You cannot stay here all night long . . . What is your name?

MÉLISANDE.

Mélisande.

GOLAUD.

You cannot stay here, Mélisande. Come with me . . .

MÉLISANDE.

I will stay here . . .

GOLAUD.

You will be afraid, all alone. We do not know what there may be here . . . all night long . . . all alone . . . it is impossible. Mélisande, come, give me your hand . . .

MÉLISANDE.

Oh, do not touch me! . . .

GOLAUD.

Do not scream . . . I will not touch you again. But come with me. The night will be very dark and very cold. Come with me . . .

MÉLISANDE.

Where are you going? . . .

GOLAUD.

I do not know . . . I am lost too . . .

[Exeunt.

SCENE III.—A hall in the castle. ARKËL and GENEVIÈVE discovered.

GENEVIÈVE.

Here is what he writes to his brother Pélléas: "I found her all in tears one evening, beside a spring in the forest where I had lost myself. I do not know her age, nor who she is, nor whence she comes, and I dare not question her, for she must have had a sore fright; and when you ask her what has happened to her, she falls at once a-weeping like a child, and sobs so heavily you are afraid. Just as I found her by the springs, a crown of gold had slipped from her hair and fallen to the bottom of the water. She was clad, besides, like a princess, though her garments had been torn by the briers. It is now six months since I married her and I know no more about it than on the day of our meeting. Meanwhile, dear Pélléas, thou whom I love more than a brother, although we were not born of the same father; meanwhile make ready for my return . . . I know my mother will willingly forgive me. But I am afraid of the King, our venerable grandsire, I am afraid of Arkël, in spite of all his kindness, for I have undone by this strange marriage all his plans of state, and I fear the beauty of Mélisande will not excuse my folly to eyes so wise as his. If he consents nevertheless to receive her as he would receive his own daughter, the third night following this letter, light a lamp at the top of the tower that overlooks the sea. I shall perceive it from the bridge of our ship; otherwise I shall go far away again and come back no more . . ." What say you of it?

ARKËL.

Nothing. He has done what he probably must have done. I am very old, and nevertheless I have not yet seen clearly for one moment into myself; how would you that I judge what others have done? I am not far from the tomb and do not succeed in judging myself . . . One always mistakes when one does not close his eyes. That may seem strange to us; but that is all. He is past the age to marry and he weds like a child, a little girl he finds by a spring . . . That may seem strange to us, because we never see but the reverse of destinies . . . the reverse even of our own . . . He has always followed my counsels hitherto; I had thought to make him happy in sending him to ask the hand of Princess Ursula . . . He could not remain alone; since the death of his wife he has been sad to be alone; and that marriage would have put an end to long wars and old hatreds . . . He would not have it so. Let it be as he would have it; I have never put myself athwart a destiny; and he knows better than I his future. There happen perhaps no useless events . . .

GENEVIÈVE.

He has always been so prudent, so grave and so firm . . . If it were Pélleas, I should understand . . . But he . . . at his age . . . Who is it he is going to introduce here?—An unknown found along the roads . . .

Since his wife's death, he has no longer lived for aught but his son, the little Yniold, and if he were about to marry again, it was because you had wished it . . . And now . . . a little girl in the forest . . . He has forgotten everything . . .—What shall we do? . . .
Enter PÉLLÉAS.

ARKËL.

Who is coming in there?

GENEVIÈVE.

It is Pélléas. He has been weeping.

ARKËL.

Is it thou, Pélléas?—Come a little nearer, that I may see thee in the light . . .

PÉLLÉAS.

Grandfather, I received another letter at the same time as my brother's; a letter from my friend Marcellus . . . He is about to die and calls for me. He would see me before dying . . .

ARKËL.

Thou wouldst leave before thy brother's return?—Perhaps thy friend is less ill than he thinks . . .

PÉLLÉAS

His letter is so sad you can see death between the lines . . . He says he knows the very day when death must come . . . He tells me I can arrive before it if I will, but that there is no more time to lose. The journey is very long, and if I await Golaud's return, it will be perhaps too late . . .

ARKËL.

Thou must wait a little while, nevertheless . . . We do not know what
this return has in store for us. And besides, is not thy father here,
above us, more sick perhaps than thy friend . . . Couldst thou choose
between the father and the friend? . . .   *[Exit.*

GENEVIÈVE.

Have a care to keep the lamp lit from this evening, Pélléas . . .

[Exeunt severally.

SCENE IV.—Before the castle. Enter GENEVIÈVE and
MÉLISANDE.

MÉLISANDE.

It is gloomy in the gardens. And what forests, what forests all about
the palaces! . . .

GENEVIÈVE.

Yes; that astonished me too when I came hither; it astonishes
everybody. There are places where you never see the sun. But one
gets used to it so quickly . . . It is long ago, it is long ago . . . It is
nearly forty years that I have lived here . . . Look toward the other
side, you will have the light of the sea . . .

MÉLISANDE.

I hear a noise below us . . .

GENEVIÈVE.

Yes; it is some one coming up toward us . . . Ah! it is Pélléas . . . He
seems still tired from having waited so long for you . . .

30

MÉLISANDE.

He has not seen us.

GENEVIÈVE.

I think he has seen us but does not know what he should do . . .
Pélléas, Pélléas, is it thou? . . .

Enter PÉLLÉAS

PÉLLÉAS.

Yes! . . . I was coming toward the sea . . .

GENEVIÈVE.

So were we; we were seeking the light. It is a little lighter here than
elsewhere; and yet the sea is gloomy.

PÉLLÉAS

We shall have a storm to-night. There has been one every night for
some time, and yet it is so calm now . . . One might embark unwittingly
and come back no more.

MÉLISANDE.

Something is leaving the port . . .

PÉLLÉAS.

It must be a big ship . . . The lights are very high, we shall see it in a
moment, when it enters the band of light . . .

GENEVIÈVE.

I do not know whether we shall be able to see it . . . there is still a fog
on the sea . . .

PÉLLÉAS.

The fog seems to be rising slowly . . .

MÉLISANDE.

Yes; I see a little light down there, which I had not seen . . .

PÉLLÉAS.

It is a lighthouse; there are others we cannot see yet.

MÉLISANDE.

The ship is in the light . . . It is already very far away . . .

PÉLLÉAS.

It is a foreign ship. It looks larger than ours . . .

MÉLISANDE.

It is the ship that brought me here! . . .

PÉLLÉAS.

It flies away under full sail . . .

MÉLISANDE.

It is the ship that brought me here. It has great sails . . . I recognized it by its sails.

PÉLLÉAS.

There will be a rough sea to-night.

MÉLISANDE.

Why does it go away to-night? . . . You can hardly see it any longer . . . Perhaps it will be wrecked . . .

PÉLLÉAS.

The sight falls very quickly . . . [*A silence.*

GENEVIÈVE.

No one speaks any more? . . . You have nothing more to say to each other? . . . It is time to go in. Pélléas, show Mélisande the way. I mast go see little Yniold a moment. [*Exit.*

PÉLLÉAS.

Nothing can be seen any longer on the sea . . .

MÉLISANDE.

I see more lights.

PÉLLÉAS.

It is the other lighthouses . . . Do you hear the sea? . . . It is the wind rising . . . Let us go down this way. Will you give me your hand?

MÉLISANDE.

See, see, my hands are full . . .

PÉLLÉAS.

I will hold you by the arm, the road is steep and it is very gloomy there . . . I am going away perhaps to-morrow . . .

MÉLISANDE.

Oh! . . . why do you go away? [*Exeunt.*

ACT SECOND.

SCENE I.—*A fountain in the park.*
Enter PÉLLÉAS and MÉLISANDE.

PÉLLÉAS.

You do not know where I have brought you?—I often come to sit here, toward noon, when it is too hot in the gardens. It is stifling to-day, even in the shade of the trees.

MÉLISANDE.

Oh, how clear the water is! . . .

PÉLLÉAS.

It is as cool as winter. It is an old abandoned spring. It seems to have been a miraculous spring,—it opened the eyes of the blind,—they still call it "Blind Man's Spring."

MÉLISANDE.

It no longer opens the eyes of the blind?

PÉLLÉAS.

Since the King has been nearly blind himself, no one comes any more . . .

MÉLISANDE.

How alone one is here! . . . There is no sound.

PÉLLÉAS.

There is always a wonderful silence here . . . One could hear the water sleep . . . Will you sit down on the edge of the marble basin? There is one linden where the sun never comes . . .

MÉLISANDE.

I am going to lie down on the marble.—I should like to see the bottom of the water . . .

PÉLLÉAS.

No one has ever seen it.—It is as deep, perhaps, as the sea.—It is not known whence it comes.—Perhaps it comes from the bottom of the earth . . .

MÉLISANDE.

If there were anything shining at the bottom, perhaps one could see it . . .

PÉLLÉAS.

Do not lean over so . . .

MÉLISANDE.

I would like to touch the water . . .

PÉLLÉAS.

Have a care of slipping . . . I will hold your hand . . .

MÉLISANDE.

No, no, I would plunge both hands in it . . . You would say my hands were sick to-day . . .

PÉLLÉAS.

Oh! oh! take care! take care! Mélisande! . . . Mélisande! . . .—Oh! your hair! . . .

MÉLISANDE (starting upright). I cannot, . . . I cannot reach it . . .

PÉLLÉAS.

Your hair dipped in the water . . .

MÉLISANDE.

Yes, it is longer than my arms . . . It is longer than I . . . [*A silence.*

PÉLLÉAS.

It was at the brink of a spring, too, that he found you?

MÉLISANDE.

Yes . . .

PÉLLÉAS.

What did he say to you?

MÉLISANDE.

Nothing;—I no longer remember . . .

PÉLLÉAS.

Was he quite near you?

MÉLISANDE.

Yes; he would have kissed me.

PÉLLÉAS.

And you would not?

MÉLISANDE.

No.

PÉLLÉAS.

Why would you not?

MÉLISANDE.

Oh! oh! I saw something pass at the bottom of the water . . .

PÉLLÉAS.

Take care! take care!—You will fall! What are you playing with?

MÉLISANDE.

With the ring he gave me . . .

PÉLLÉAS.

Take care; you will lose it . . .

MÉLISANDE.

No, no; I am sure of my hands . . .

PÉLLÉAS.

Do not play so, over so deep a water . . .

MÉLISANDE.

My hands do not tremble.

PÉLLÉAS.

How it shines in the sunlight I—Do not throw it so high in the air . . .

MÉLISANDE.

Oh! . . .

PÉLLÉAS.

It has fallen?

MÉLISANDE.

It has fallen into the water! . . .

PÉLLÉAS.

Where is it? where is it? . . .

MÉLISANDE.

I do not see it sink? . . .

PÉLLÉAS.

I think I see it shine . . .

MÉLISANDE.

My ring?

PÉLLÉAS.

Yes, yes; down yonder . . .

MÉLISANDE.

Oh! oh! It is so far away from us! . . . no, no, that is not it . . . that is not it . . . It is lost . . . lost . . . There is nothing any more but a great circle on the water . . . What shall we do? What shall we do now? . . .

PÉLLÉAS.

You need not be so troubled for a ring. It is nothing . . . We shall find it again, perhaps. Or else we will find another . . .

MÉLISANDE.

No, no; we shall never find it again; we shall never find any others either . . . And yet I thought I had it in my hands . . . I had already shut my hands, and it is fallen in spite of all . . . I threw it too high, toward the sun . . .

PÉLLÉAS.

Come, come, we will come back another day; . . . come, it is time. They will come to meet us. It was striking noon at the moment the ring fell.

MÉLISANDE.

What shall we say to Golaud if he ask where it is?

PÉLLÉAS.

The truth, the truth, the truth . . .   [Exeunt.

SCENE II.—An apartment in the castle. GOLAUD discovered, stretched upon his bed; MÉLISANDE, by his bedside.

GOLAUD.

Ah! ah! all goes well; it will amount to nothing. But I cannot understand how it came to pass. I was hunting quietly in the forest. All at once my horse ran away, without cause. Did he see anything unusual? . . . I had just heard the twelve strokes of noon. At the twelfth stroke he suddenly took fright and ran like a blind madman against a tree. I heard no more. I do not yet know what happened. I fell, and he must have fallen on me. I thought I had the whole forest on my breast; I thought my heart was crushed. But my heart is sound. It is nothing, apparently . . .

MÉLISANDE.

Would you like a little water?

GOLAUD.

Thanks, thanks; I am not thirsty.

MÉLISANDE.

Would you like another pillow? . . . There is a little spot of blood on this.

GOLAUD.

No, no; it is not worth while. I bled at the mouth just now. I shall bleed again perhaps . . .

MÉLISANDE.

Are you quite sure? . . . You are not suffering too much?

GOLAUD.

No, no; I have seen a good many more like this. I was made of iron and blood . . . These are not the little bones of a child; do not alarm yourself . . .

MÉLISANDE.

Close your eyes and try to sleep. I shall stay here all night . . .

GOLAUD.

No, no; I do not wish you to tire yourself so. I do not need anything; I shall sleep like a child . . . What is the matter, Mélisande? Why do you weep all at once? . . .

MÉLISANDE (bursting into tears).

I am . . . I am ill too . . .

GOLAUD.

Thou art ill? . . . What ails thee, then; what ails thee, Mélisande? . . .

MÉLISANDE.

I do not know . . . I am ill here . . . I had rather tell you to-day; my lord, my lord, I am not happy here . . .

GOLAUD.

Why, what has happened, Mélisande? What is it? . . . And I suspecting nothing . . . What has happened? . . . Some one has done thee harm? . . . Some one has given thee offence?

MÉLISANDE.

No, no; no one has done me the least harm . . . It is not that . . . It is not that . . . But I can live here no longer. I do not know why . . . I would go away, go away! . . . I shall die if I am left here . . .

GOLAUD.

But something has happened? You must be hiding something from me? . . . Tell me the whole truth, Mélisande . . . Is it the King? . . . Is it my mother? . . . Is it Pélléas? . . .

MÉLISANDE.

No, no; it is not Pélléas. It is not anybody . . . You could not understand me . . .

GOLAUD.

Why should I not understand? . . . If you tell me nothing, what will you have me do? . . . Tell me everything and I shall understand everything.

MÉLISANDE.

I do not know myself what it is . . . I do not know just what it is . . . If I could tell you, I would tell you . . . It is something stronger than I . . .

GOLAUD.

Come; be reasonable, Mélisande.—What would you have me do?—
You are no longer a child.—Is it I whom you would leave?

MÉLISANDE.

Oh! no, no; it is not that . . . I would go away with you . . . It is here that
I can live no longer . . . I feel that I shall not live a long while . . .

GOLAUD.

But there must be a reason nevertheless. You will be thought mad.
It will be thought child's dreams.—Come, is it Pélléas, perhaps?—I
think he does not often speak to you.

MÉLISANDE.

Yes, yes; he speaks to me sometimes. I think he does not like me;
I have seen it in his eyes . . . But he speaks to me when he meets
me . . .

GOLAUD.

You must not take it ill of him. He has always been so. He is a little
strange. And just now he is sad; he thinks of his friend Marcellus,
who is at the point of death, and whom he cannot go to see . . . He
will change, he will change, you will see; he is young . . .

MÉLISANDE.

But it is not that . . . it is not that . . .

GOLAUD.

What is it, then?—Can you not get used to the life one leads here?
Is it too gloomy here?—It is true the castle is very old and very
sombre . . . It is very cold, and very deep. And all those who dwell in
it, are already old. And the country may seem gloomy too, with all its

forests, all its old forests without light. But that may all be enlivened if we will. And then, joy, joy, one does not have it every day; we must take things as they come. But tell me something; no matter what; I will do everything you could wish . . .

MÉLISANDE.

Yes, yes; it is true . . . You never see the sky here. I saw it for the first time this morning . . .

GOLAUD.

It is that, then, that makes you weep, my poor Mélisande?—It is only that, then?—You weep, not to see the sky?—Come, come, you are no longer at the age when one may weep for such things . . . And then, is not the summer yonder? You will see the sky every day.—And then, next year . . . Come, give me your hand; give me both your little hands. [*He takes her hands.*] Oh! oh! these little hands that I could crush like flowers . . .—Hold! where is the ring I gave you?

MÉLISANDE.

The ring?

GOLAUD.

Yes; our wedding-ring, where is it?

MÉLISANDE.

I think . . . I think it has fallen . . .

GOLAUD.

Fallen?—Where has it fallen?—You have not lost it?

MÉLISANDE.

No, no; it fell . . . it must have fallen . . . But I know where it is . . .

GOLAUD.

Where is it?

MÉLISANDE.

You know . . . you know well . . . the grotto by the seashore? . . .

GOLAUD.

Yes.

MÉLISANDE.

Well then, it is there . . . It must be it is there . . . Yes, yes; I remember . . . I went there this morning to pick up shells for little Yniold . . . There were some very fine ones . . . It slipped from my finger . . . then the sea came in; and I had to go out before I had found it.

GOLAUD.

Are you sure it is there?

MÉLISANDE.

Yes, yes; quite sure . . . I felt it slip . . . then, all at once, the noise of the waves . . .

GOLAUD.

You must go look for it at once.

MÉLISANDE.

I must go look for it at once?

GOLAUD.

Yes.

MÉLISANDE.

Now?—at once?—in the dark?

GOLAUD.

Now, at once, in the dark. You must go look for it at once. I had rather have lost all I have than have lost that ring. You do not know what it is. You do not know whence it came. The sea will be very high to-night. The sea will come to take it before you . . . Make haste. You must go look for it at once . . .

MÉLISANDE.

I dare not . . . I dare not go alone . . .

GOLAUD.

Go, go with no matter whom. But you must go at once, do you understand?—Make haste; ask Pélléas to go with you.

MÉLISANDE.

Pélléas?—With Pélléas?—But Pélléas would not . . .

GOLAUD.

Pélléas will do all you ask of him. I know Pélléas better than you do. Go, go; hurry! I shall not sleep until I have the ring.

MÉLISANDE.

Oh! oh! I am not happy! . . . I am not happy! . . .
[Exit, weeping.
SCENE III.—*Before a grotto.*

Enter PÉLLÉAS and MÉLISANDE.

[Speaking with great agitation.] Yes; it is here; we are there. It is so dark you cannot tell the entrance of the grotto from the rest of the night . . . There are no stars on this side. Let us wait till the moon has torn through that great cloud; it will light up the whole grotto, and then we can enter without danger. There are dangerous places, and the path is very narrow between two lakes whose bottom has not yet been found. I did not think to bring a torch or a lantern, but I think the light of the sky will be enough for us.—You have never gone into this grotto?

MÉLISANDE.

No . . .

PÉLLÉAS.

Let us go in; let us go in . . . You must be able to describe the place where you lost the ring, if he questions you . . . It is very big and very beautiful. There are stalactites that look like plants and men. It is full of blue darks. It has not yet been explored to the end. There are great treasures hidden there, it seems. You will see the remains of ancient shipwrecks there. But you must not go far in it without a guide. There have been some who never have come back. I myself dare not go forward too far. We will stop the moment we no longer see the light of the sea or the sky. When you strike a little light there, you would say the vault was covered with stars like the sky. It is bits of crystal or salt, they say, that shine so in the rock.—Look, look, I think the sky is going to clear . . . Give me your hand; do not tremble, do not tremble so. There is no danger; we will stop the moment we no longer see the light of the sea . . . Is it the noise of the grotto that frightens you? It is the noise of night or the noise of silence . . . Do you hear the sea behind us?—It does not seem happy to-night . . . Ah! look, the light! . . .

[The moon lights up abundantly the entrance and part of the darkness of the grotto; and at a certain depth are seen three old beggars with white hair, seated side by side, leaning upon each other and asleep against a bowlder.]

MÉLISANDE.

Ah!

PÉLLÉAS.

What is it?

MÉLISANDE.

There are . . . there are . . .
[She points out the three Beggars.

PÉLLÉAS.

Yes, yes; I have seen them too . . .

MÉLISANDE.

Let us go! . . . Let us go! . . .

PÉLLÉAS.

Yes . . . it is three old poor men fallen asleep . . . There is a famine in the country . . . Why have they come to sleep here . . .

MÉLISANDE.

Let us go! . . . Come, come . . . Let us go! . . .

PÉLLÉAS.

Take care; do not speak so loud . . . Let us not wake them . . . They are still sleeping heavily . . . Come.

MÉLISANDE.

Leave me, leave me; I prefer to walk alone . . .

PÉLLÉAS.

We will come back another day . . .   *[Exeunt.*

SCENE IV.—An apartment in the castle, ARKËL and PÉLLÉAS discovered.

ARKËL.

You see that everything retains you here just now and forbids you this useless journey. We have concealed your father's condition from you until now; but it is perhaps hopeless; and that alone should suffice to stop you on the threshold. But there are so many other reasons . . . And it is not in the day when our enemies awake, and when the people are dying of hunger and murmur about us, that you have the right to desert us. And why this journey? Marcellus is dead; and life has graver duties than the visit to a tomb. You are weary, you say, of your inactive life; but activity and duty are not found on the highways. They must be waited for upon the threshold, and let in as they go by; and they go by every day. You have never seen them? I hardly see them any more myself; but I will teach you to see them, and I will point them out to you the day when you would make them a sign. Nevertheless, listen to me; if you believe it is from the depths of your life this journey is exacted, I do not forbid your undertaking it, for you must know better than I the events you must offer to your being or your fate. I shall ask you only to wait until we know what must take place ere long . . .

PÉLLÉAS.

How long must I wait?

ARKËL.

    A few weeks; perhaps a few days . . .

PÉLLÉAS.

    I will wait . . .

ACT THIRD

    SCENE I.—An apartment in the castle. PÉLLÉAS and MÉLISANDE discovered, MÉLISANDE plies her distaff at the back of the room.

PÉLLÉAS.

    Yniold does not come back; where has he gone?

MÉLISANDE

    He had heard something in the corridor; he has gone to see what it is.

PÉLLÉAS.

    Mélisande . . .

MÉLISANDE

    What is it?

PÉLLÉAS.

    . . . Can you see still to work there? . . .

MÉLISANDE

    I work as well in the dark . . .

PÉLLÉAS.

I think everybody is already asleep in the castle. Golaud does not come back from the chase. It is late, nevertheless . . . He no longer suffers from his fall? . . .

MÉLISANDE.

He said he no longer suffered from it.

PÉLLÉAS.

He must be more prudent; his body is no longer as supple as at twenty years . . . I see the stars through the window and the light of the moon on the trees. It is late; he will not come back now. [*Knocking at the door.*] Who is there? . . . Come in! . . .
Little YNIOLD *opens the door and enters the room.*
It was you knocking so? . . . That is not the way to knock at doors. It is as if a misfortune had arrived; look, you have frightened little mother.

LITTLE YNIOLD.

I only knocked a tiny little bit.

PÉLLÉAS.

It is late; little father will not come back to-night; it is time for you to go to bed.

LITTLE YNIOLD.

I shall not go to bed before you do.

PÉLLÉAS.

What? . . . What is that you are saying?

LITTLE YNIOLD.

I say ... not before you ... not before you ...

[*Bursts into sobs and takes refuge by MÉLISANDE.*]

MÉLISANDE.

What is it, Yniold? ... What is it? ... why do you weep all at once?

YNIOLD *(sobbing)*.

Because ... oh! oh! because ...

MÉLISANDE.

Because what? ... Because what? ... Tell me ...

YNIOLD.

Little mother ... little mother ... you are going away ...

MÉLISANDE.

But what has taken hold of you, Yniold? ... I have never dreamed of going away ...

YNIOLD.

Yes, you have; yes, you have; little father has gone away ... Little father does not come back, and you are going to go away too ... I have seen it ... I have seen it ...

MÉLISANDE.

But there has never been any idea of that, Yniold ... Why, what makes you think that I would go away? ...

YNIOLD.

I have seen it ... I have seen it ... You have said things to uncle that I could not hear ...

PÉLLÉAS.

He is sleepy ... He has been dreaming ... Come here, Yniold; asleep already? ... Come and look out at the window; the swans are fighting with the dogs ...

YNIOLD *(at the window).*

Oh! oh! they are chasing the dogs! ... They are chasing them! ... Oh! oh! the water! ... the wings! ... the wings! ... they are afraid ...

PÉLLÉAS. (coming back by MÉLISANDE).

He is sleepy; he is struggling against sleep; his eyes were closing ...

MÉLISANDE (singing softly as she spins).
Saint Daniel and Saint Michaël ...
Saint Michaël and Saint Raphaël ...

YNIOLD *(at the window).*
Oh! oh! little mother! ...

MÉLISANDE (rising abruptly).
What is it, Yniold? ... What is it? ...

YNIOLD.
I saw something at the window? ...

[PÉLLÉAS and MÉLISANDE run to the window.

PÉLLÉAS.

What is there at the window? . . . What have you seen? . . .

YNIOLD.

Oh! oh! I saw something! . . .

PÉLLÉAS.

But there is nothing. I see nothing . . .

MÉLISANDE.

Nor I . . .

PÉLLÉAS.

Where did you see something? Which way? . . .

YNIOLD.

Down there, down there! . . . It is no longer there . . .

PÉLLÉAS.

He does not know what he is saying. He must have seen the light of the moon on the forest. There are often strange reflections, . . . or else something must have passed on the highway . . . or in his sleep. For see, see, I believe he is quite asleep . . .

YNIOLD (at the window).

Little father is there! little father is there!

PÉLLÉAS (going to the window).

He is right; Golaud is coming into the courtyard . . .

YNIOLD.

Little father! . . . little father! . . . I am going to meet him! . . .

[Exit, running,—A silence.

PÉLLÉAS.

They are coming up the stair . . .

Enter GOLAUD and little YNIOLD with a lamp.

GOLAUD.

You are still waiting in the dark?

YNIOLD.

I have brought a light, little mother, a big light! . . . [*He lifts the lamp and looks at MÉLISANDE.*] You have been weeping, little mother? . . . You have been, weeping? . . . [He lifts the lamp toward PÉLLÉAS and looks in turn at him.] You too, you too, you have been weeping? . . . Little father, look, little father; they have both been weeping . . .

GOLAUD.

Do not hold the light under their eyes so . . .

SCENE II.—*One of the towers of the castle.—watchman's round passes under a window in the tower.*

MÉLISANDE (at the window, combing her unbound hair).

My long locks fall foaming
To the threshold of the tower,—
My locks await your coming
All along the tower,
And all the long, long hour,
And all the long, long hour.
Saint Daniel and Saint Michaël,
Saint Michaël and Saint Raphaël.

I was born on a Sunday,
A Sunday at high noon . . .

Enter PÉLLÉAS *by the watchman's round.*

PÉLLÉAS.

Holà! Holà! ho! . . .

MÉLISANDE.

Who is there?

PÉLLÉAS.

I, I, and I! . . . What art thou doing there at the window, singing like a
bird that is not native here?

MÉLISANDE.

I am doing my hair for the night . . .

PÉLLÉAS.

Is it that I see upon the wall? . . . I thought you had some light . . .

MÉLISANDE.

I have opened the window; it is too hot in the tower . . . It is beautiful
to-night . . .

PÉLLÉAS.

There are innumerable stars; I have never seen so many as to-night; . . .
but the moon is still upon the sea . . . Do not stay in the shadow,
Mélisande; lean forward a little till I see your unbound hair . . .

MÉLISANDE.

I am frightful so . . .

[She learn out at the window.

PÉLLÉAS.

Oh! oh! Mélisande! . . . oh, thou art beautiful! . . . thou art beautiful so! . . . Lean out! lean out! . . . Let me come nearer thee . . .

MÉLISANDE

I cannot come nearer thee . . . I am leaning out as far as I can . . .

PÉLLÉAS.

I cannot come up higher; . . . give me at least thy hand to-night . . . before I go away . . . I leave to-morrow . . .

MÉLISANDE.

No, no, no! . . .

PÉLLÉAS.

Yes, yes, yes; I leave, I shall leave to-morrow . . . Give me thy hand, thy hand, thy little hand upon my lips . . .

MÉLISANDE.

I give thee not my hand if thou wilt leave . . .

PÉLLÉAS.

Give, give, give! . . .

MÉLISANDE.

Thou wilt not leave? . . .

PÉLLÉAS.

I will wait; I will wait . . .

MÉLISANDE.

I see a rose in the shadows . . .

PÉLLÉAS.

Where? . . . I see only the boughs of the willow hanging over the wall . . .

MÉLISANDE.

Further down, further down, in the garden; further down, in the sombre green . . .

PÉLLÉAS.

It is not a rose . . . I will go see by and by, but give me thy hand first; first thy hand . . .

MÉLISANDE.

There, there; . . . I cannot lean out further . . .

PÉLLÉAS.

I cannot reach thy hand with my lips . . .

MÉLISANDE.

I cannot lean out further . . . I am on the point of falling . . .—Oh! oh! my hair is falling down the tower! . . .

[Her tresses fall suddenly over her head, as she is leaning out so, and stream over PÉLLÉAS]

PÉLLÉAS.

Oh! oh! what is it? . . . Thy hair, thy hair is falling down to me! . . . All thy locks, Mélisande, all thy locks have fallen down the tower! . . . I hold them in my hands; I hold them in my mouth . . . I hold them in my arms; I put them about my neck . . . I will not open my hands again to-night . . .

MÉLISANDE.

Let me go! let me go! . . . Thou wilt make me fall! . . .

PÉLLÉAS.

No, no, no; . . . I have never seen such hair as thine, Mélisande! . . . See, see, see; it comes from so high and yet it floods me to the heart! . . . And yet it floods me to the knees! . . . And it is sweet, sweet as if it fell from heaven! . . . I see the sky no longer through thy locks. Thou seest, thou seest? . . . I can no longer hold them with both hands; there are some on the boughs of the willow . . . They are alive like birds in my hands, . . . and they love me, they love me more than thou! . . .

MÉLISANDE.

Let me go; let me go! . . . Some one might come . . .

PÉLLÉAS.

No, no, no; I shall not set thee free to-night . . . Thou art my prisoner to-night; all night, all night! . . .

MÉLISANDE.

Pélléas! Pélléas! . . .

PÉLLÉAS.

I tie them, I tie them to the willow boughs . . . Thou shalt not go away now; . . . thou shalt not go away now . . . Look, look, I am kissing thy hair . . . I suffer no more in the midst of thy hair . . . Hearest thou my kisses along thy hair? . . . They mount along thy hair . . . Each hair must bring thee some . . . Thou seest, thou seest, I can open my hands . . . My hands are free, and thou canst not leave me now . . .

MÉLISANDE.

Oh! oh! thou hurtest me . . . [*Doves come out of the tower and fly about them in the night.*]—What is that, Pélléas?—What is it flying about me?

PÉLLÉAS.

It is the doves coming oat of the tower . . . I have frightened them; they are flying away . . .

MÉLISANDE.

It is my doves, Pélléas.—Let us go away, let me go; they will not come back again . . .

PÉLLÉAS.

Why will they not come back again?

MÉLISANDE

They will be lost in the dark . . . Let me go; let me lift my head . . . I hear a noise of footsteps . . . Let me go!—It is Golaud! . . . I believe it is Golaud! . . . He has heard us . . .

PÉLLÉAS.

Wait! Wait! . . . Thy hair is about the boughs . . . It is caught there in the darkness . . . Wait, wait! . . . It is dark . . .

Enter GOLAUD, by the watchman's round.

GOLAUD.

What do you here?

59

PÉLLÉAS.

What do I here? . . . I . . .

GOLAUD.

You are children . . . Mélisande, do not lean out so at the window; you
will fall . . . Do you not know it is late?—It is nearly midnight.—Do
not play so in the darkness.—You are children . . . *[Laughing nervously.]*
What children! . . . What children! . . .

[Exit, with PÉLLÉAS.

SCENE III.—*The-vaults of the castle.*

Enter GOLAUD and PÉLLÉAS.

GOLAUD.

Take care; this way, this way.—You have never penetrated into these
vaults?

PÉLLÉAS.

Yes; once, of old; but it was long ago . . .

GOLAUD.

They are prodigious great; it is a succession of enormous crypts that
end, God knows where. The whole castle is builded on these crypts. Do
you smell the deathly odor that reigns here?—That is what I wished,
to show you. In my opinion, it comes from the little underground
lake I am going to have you see. Take care; walk before me, in the
light of my lantern. I will warn you when we are there, *[They continue
to walk in silence.]* Hey! hey! Pélléas! stop! stop!—*[He seizes him by the
arm.]* For God's sake! . . . Do you not see?—One step more, and you
had been in the gulf! . . .

PÉLLÉAS

But I did not see it! . . . The lantern no longer lighted me . . .

GOLAUD.

I made a misstep . . . but if I had not held you by the arm . . . Well, this is the stagnant water that I spoke of to you . . . Do you perceive the smell of death that rises?—Let us go to the end of this overhanging rock, and do you lean over a little. It will strike you in the face.

PÉLLÉAS.

I smell it already; . . . you would say a smell of the tomb.

GOLAUD.

Further, further . . . It is this that on certain days has poisoned the castle. The King will not believe it comes from here.—The crypt should be walled up in which this standing water is found. It is time, besides, to examine these vaults a little. Have you noticed those lizards on the walls and pillars of the vaults?—There is a labor hidden here you would not suspect; and the whole castle will be swallowed up one of these nights, if it is not looked out for. But what will you have? nobody likes to come down this far . . . There are strange lizards in many of the walls . . . Oh! here . . . do you perceive the smell of death that rises?

PÉLLÉAS.

Yes; there is a smell of death rising about us . . .

GOLAUD.

Lean over; have no fear . . . I will hold you . . . give me . . . no, no, not your hand . . . it might slip . . . your arm, your arm! . . . Do you see the gulf? [*Moved.*]—Pélléas? Pélléas? . . .

PÉLLÉAS.

Yes; I think I see the bottom of the gulf . . . Is it the light that trembles so? . . . You . . . [*He straightens up, turns, and looks at GOLAUD.*]

GOLAUD (with a trembling voice).

Yes; it is the lantern . . . See, I shook it to lighten the walls . . .

PÉLLÉAS.

I stifle here; . . . let us go out . . .

GOLAUD.

Yes; let us go out . . .

[*Exeunt in silence.*

SCENE IV.—A terrace at the exit of the vaults. Enter GOLAUD and PÉLLÉAS.

PÉLLÉAS.

Ah! I breathe at last! . . . I thought, one moment, I was going to be ill in those enormous crypts; I was on the point of falling . . . There is a damp air there, heavy as a leaden dew, and darkness thick as a poisoned paste . . . And now, all the air of all the sea! . . . There is a fresh wind, see; fresh as a leaf that has just opened, over the little green waves . . . Hold! the flowers have just been watered at the foot of the terrace, and the smell of the verdure and the wet roses comes up to us . . . It must be nearly noon; they are already in the shadow of the tower . . . It is noon; I hear the bells ringing, and the children are going down to the beach to bathe . . . I did not know that we had stayed so long in the caverns . . .

GOLAUD.

We went down towards eleven o'clock . . .

PÉLLÉAS.

Earlier; it must have been earlier; I heard it strike half-past ten.

GOLAUD.

Half-past ten or a quarter to eleven . . .

PÉLLÉAS.

They have opened all the windows of the castle. It will be unusually hot this afternoon . . . Look, there is mother with Mélisande at a window of the tower . . .

GOLAUD.

Yes; they have taken refuge on the shady side.—Speaking of Mélisande, I heard what passed and what was said last night. I am quite aware all that is but child's play; but it need not be repeated. Mélisande is very young and very impressionable; and she must be treated the more circumspectly that she is perhaps with child at this moment . . . She is very delicate, hardly woman; and the least emotion might bring on a mishap. It is not the first time I have noticed there might be something between you . . . You are older than she; it will suffice to have told you . . . Avoid her as much as possible; without affectation moreover; without affectation . . .—What is it I see yonder on the highway toward the forest? . . .

PÉLLÉAS.

Some herds they are leading to the city . . .

GOLAUD.

They cry like lost children; you would say they smelt the butcher already.—It will be time for dinner.—What a fine day! What a capital day for the harvest! . . .

[Exeunt.

SCENE V.—*Before the castle.*

Enter GOLAUD and little YNIOLD.

GOLAUD.

Come, we are going to sit down here, Yniold; sit on my knee; we shall see from here what passes in the forest. I do not see you any more at all now. You abandon me too; you are always at little mother's . . . Why, we are sitting just under little mother's windows.—Perhaps she is saying her evening prayer at this moment . . . But tell me, Yniold, she is often with your uncle Pélléas, isn't she?

YNIOLD.

Yes, yes; always, little father; when you are not there, little father . . .

GOLAUD.

Ah!—look; some one is going by with a lantern in the garden.—But I have been told they did not like each other . . . It seems they often quarrel; . . . no? Is it true?

YNIOLD.

Yes, yes; it is true.

GOLAUD.

Yes?—Ah! ah!—But what do they quarrel about?

64

YNIOLD.

About the door.

GOLAUD.

What? about the door?—What are you talking about?—No, come, explain yourself; why do they quarrel about the door?

YNIOLD.

Because it won't stay open.

GOLAUD.

Who wants it to stay open?—Come, why do they quarrel?

YNIOLD.

I don't know, little father; about the light.

GOLAUD.

I am not talking to you about the light; we will talk of that by and by. I am talking to you about the door. Answer what I ask you; you must learn to talk; it is time . . . Do not put your hand in your mouth so; . . . come . . .

YNIOLD.

Little father! little father! . . . I won't do it any more . . . [*He cries.*]

GOLAUD.

Come; what are you crying for now? What has happened?

YNIOLD.

Oh! oh! little father, you hurt me . . .

GOLAUD.

I hurt you?—Where did I hurt you? I did not mean to . . .

YNIOLD.

Here, here; on my little arm . . .

GOLAUD.

I did not mean to; come, don't cry any more, and I will give you something to-morrow.

YNIOLD.

What, little father?

GOLAUD.

A quiver and some arrows; but tell me what you know about the door.

YNIOLD.

Big arrows?

GOLAUD.

Yes, yes; very big arrows.—But why don't they want the door to be open?—Come, answer me sometime!—no, no; do not open your mouth to cry. I am not angry. We are going to have a quiet talk, like Pélléas and little mother when they are together. What do they talk about when they are together?

YNIOLD.

Pélléas and little mother?

GOLAUD.

Yes; what do they talk about?

YNIOLD.

About me; always about me.

GOLAUD.

And what do they say about you?

YNIOLD.

They say I am going to be very big.

GOLAUD.

Oh, plague of my life! . . . I am here like a blind man searching for his treasure at the bottom of the ocean! . . . I am here like a new-born child lost in the forest, and you . . . Come, come, Yniold, I was wandering; we are going to talk seriously. Do Pélléas and little mother never speak of me when I am not there? . . .

YNIOLD.

Yes, yes, little father; they are always speaking of you.

GOLAUD.

Ah! . . . And what do they say of me?

YNIOLD.

They say I shall grow as big as you are.

GOLAUD.

You are always by them?

YNIOLD.

Yes, yes, always, always, little father.

GOLAUD.

They never tell you to go play somewhere else?

YNIOLD.

No, little father; they are afraid when I am not there.

GOLAUD.

They are afraid? . . . What makes you think they are afraid?

YNIOLD.

Little mother always says, "Don't go away; don't go away!" . . . They are unhappy, but they laugh . . .

GOLAUD.

But that does not prove they are afraid.

YNIOLD.

Yes, yes, little father; she is afraid . . .

GOLAUD.

Why do you say she is afraid?

YNIOLD.

They always weep in the dark.

GOLAUD.

Ah! ah! . . .

YNIOLD.

That makes one weep too.

GOLAUD.

Yes, yes! . . .

YNIOLD.

She is pale, little father.

GOLAUD.

Ah! ah! . . . patience, my God, patience! . . .

YNIOLD.

What, little father?

GOLAUD.

Nothing, nothing, my child.—I saw a wolf go by in the forest.—
Then they get on well together?—I am glad to learn they are on good
terms.—They kiss each other sometimes—No? . . .

YNIOLD.

Kiss each other, little father?—No, no,—ah! yes, little father, yes; yes;
once . . . once when it rained . . .

GOLAUD.

They kissed?—But how, how did they kiss?

YNIOLD.

So, little father, so! . . . *[He gives him a kiss on the mouth, laughing.]* Ah! ah!
your beard, little father! . . . It pricks! it pricks! it pricks! It is getting all
gray, little father, and your hair, too; all gray, all gray, all gray . . . *[The
window under which they are sitting is lighted up at this moment, and the light
falls upon them.]* Ah! ah! little mother has lit her lamp. It is light, little
father; it is light . . .

GOLAUD.

Yes; it is beginning to be light . . .

YNIOLD.

Let us go there too, little father; let us go there too . . .

GOLAUD.

Where do you want to go?

YNIOLD.

Where it is light, little father.

GOLAUD.

No, no, my child; let us stay in the dark a little longer . . . One cannot tell, one cannot tell yet . . . Do you see those poor people down there trying to kindle a little fire in the forest?—It has rained. And over there, do you see the old gardener trying to lift that tree the wind has blown down across the road?—He cannot; the tree is too big; the tree is too heavy, and it will lie where it fell. All that cannot be helped . . . I think Pélléas is mad . . .

YNIOLD.

No, little father, he is not mad; he is very good.

GOLAUD.

Do you want to see little mother?

YNIOLD.

Yes, yes; I want to see her!

GOLAUD.

Don't make any noise; I am going to hoist you up to the window. It is too high for me, for all I am so big . . . *[He lifts the child.]* Do not make the least noise; little mother would be terribly afraid . . . Do you see her?—Is she in the room?

YNIOLD.

Yes . . . Oh, how light it is!

GOLAUD.

She is alone?

YNIOLD.

Yes; . . . no, no; Uncle Pélléas Is there, too.

GOLAUD.

He—. . . !

YNIOLD.

Ah! ah! little father! you have hurt me! . . .

GOLAUD.

It is nothing; be still; I will not do it any more; look, look, Yniold! . . . I stumbled; speak lower. What are they doing?—

YNIOLD.

They are not doing anything, little father; they are waiting for something.

GOLAUD.

Are they near each other?

YNIOLD.

No, little father.

GOLAUD.

And . . . and the bed? are they near the bed?

YNIOLD.

The bed, little father?—I can't see the bed.

GOLAUD.

Lower, lower; they will hear you. Are they speaking?

YNIOLD.

No, little father; they do not speak.

GOLAUD.

But what are they doing?—They must be doing something . . .

YNIOLD.

They are looking at the light.

GOLAUD.

Both?

YNIOLD.

Yes, little father.

GOLAUD.

They do not say anything?

YNIOLD.

No, little father; they do not close their eyes.

GOLAUD.

They do not come near each other?

YNIOLD.

No, little father; they do not stir.

GOLAUD.

They are sitting down?

YNIOLD.

No, little father; they are standing upright against the wall.

GOLAUD.

They make no gestures?—They do not look at each other?—They make no signs? . . .

YNIOLD.

No, little father.—Oh! oh! little father; they never close their eyes . . . I am terribly afraid . . .

GOLAUD.

Be still. They do not stir yet?

YNIOLD.

No, little father.—I am afraid, little father; let me come down! . . .

GOLAUD.

Why, what are you afraid of?—Look! look! . . .

YNIOLD.

I dare not look any more, little father! . . . Let me come down! . . .

GOLAUD.

Look! look! . . .

YNIOLD.

Oh! oh! I am going to cry, little father!—Let me come down! let me
come down!,.

GOLAUD.

Come; we will go see what has happened.

[Exeunt.

ACT FOURTH

SCENE I.—*A corridor in the castle.*

Enter PÉLLÉAS and MÉLISANDE, meeting.

PÉLLÉAS.

Where goest thou? I must speak to thee to-night. Shall I see thee?

MÉLISANDE.

Yes.

PÉLLÉAS.

I have just left my father's room. He is getting better. The physician
has told us he is saved . . . And yet this morning I had a presentiment
this day would end ill. I have had a rumor of misfortune in my ears
for some time . . . Then, all at once there was a great change; to-day it

is no longer anything but a question of time. All the windows in his room have been thrown open. He speaks; he seems happy. He does not speak yet like an ordinary man, but already his ideas no longer all come from the other world . . . He recognized me. He took my hand and said with that strange air he has had since he fell sick: "Is it thou, Pélléas? Why, why, I had not noticed it before, but thou hast the grave and friendly look of those who will not live long . . . You must travel; you must travel . . ." It is strange; I shall obey him . . . My mother listened to him and wept for joy.—Hast thou not been aware of it?—The whole house seems already to revive, you hear breathing, you hear speaking, you hear walking . . . Listen; I hear some one speaking behind that door. Quick, quick! answer quickly! where shall I see thee?

MÉLISANDE.

Where wouldst thou?

PÉLLÉAS.

In the park; near "Blind Man's Spring."—Wilt thou?—Wilt thou come?

MÉLISANDE.

Yes.

PÉLLÉAS.

It will be the last night;—I am going to travel, as my father said. Thou wilt not see me more . . .

MÉLISANDE.

Do not say that, Pélléas . . . I shall see thee always; I shall look upon thee always . . .

PÉLLÉAS.

Thou wilt look in vain . . . I shall be so far away thou couldst no longer see me . . . I shall try to go very far away . . . I am full of joy, and you would say I had all the weight of heaven and earth on my body to-day . . .

MÉLISANDE.

What has happened, Pélléas?—I no longer understand what you say . . .

PÉLLÉAS.

Go, go; let us separate. I hear some one speaking behind that door . . . It is the strangers who came to the castle this morning . . . They are going out . . . Let us go; it is the strangers . . . *[Exeunt severally.*

SCENE II.—An apartment in the castle. ARKËL and MÉLISANDE discovered.

ARKËL.

Now that Pélléas's father is saved, and sickness, the old handmaid of Death, has left the castle, a little joy and a little sunlight will at last come into the house again . . . It was time!—For, since thy coming, we have only lived here whispering about a closed room . . . And truly I have pitied thee, Mélisande . . . Thou camest here all joyous, like a child seeking a gala-day, and at the moment thou enteredst in the vestibule I saw thy face change, and probably thy soul, as the face changes in spite of us when we enter at noon into a grotto too gloomy and too cold . . . And since,—since, on account of all that, I have often no longer understood thee . . . I observed thee, thou went there, listless perhaps, but with the strange, astray look of one awaiting ever a great trouble, in the sunlight, in a beautiful garden . . . I cannot explain . . . But I was sad to see thee so; for thou art too young and too beautiful to live already day and night under the breath of death . . . But now all that will change. At my age,—and there perhaps is the surest fruit of my life,—at my age I have gained I know not what faith in the fidelity of events, and I have always seen that every young and beautiful being creates about itself young, beautiful, and happy events . . . And it is thou who wilt now open the door for the new era I have glimpses of . . . Come here; why dost thou stay there without answering and without lifting thine eyes?—I have kissed thee but once only hitherto,—the day of thy coming; and yet old men need sometimes to touch with their lips a woman's forehead or a child's cheek, to believe still in the freshness of life and avert awhile the menaces . . . Art thou afraid of my old lips? How I have pitied thee these months! . . .

MÉLISANDE.

Grandfather, I have not been unhappy . . .

ARKËL.

Perhaps you were of those who are unhappy without knowing it, . . . and they are the most unhappy . . . Let me look at thee, so, quite near, a moment; . . . we have such need of beauty beside Death . . .

Enter GOLAUD.

GOLAUD.

Pélléas leaves to-night.

ARKËL.

Thou hast blood on thy forehead.—What hast thou done?

GOLAUD.

Nothing, nothing . . . I have passed through a hedge of thorns.

MÉLISANDE.

Bend down your head a little, my lord . . . I will wipe your forehead . . .

GOLAUD (repulsing her).

I will not that you touch me, do you understand? Go, go!—I am not speaking to you.—Where is my sword?—I came to seek my sword . . .

MÉLISANDE.

Here; on the praying-stool.

GOLAUD.

Bring it. [*To ARKËL.*]—They have just found another peasant dead of hunger, along by the sea. You would say they all meant to die under our eyes.—[*To MÉLISANDE.*] Well, my sword?—Why do you tremble so?—I am not going to kill you. I would simply examine the blade. I do not employ the sword for these uses. Why do you examine me like a beggar?—I do not come to ask alms of you. You hope to see something in my eyes without my seeing anything in yours?—Do you think I may know something?—[*To ARKËL.*]—Do you see those great eyes?—It is as if they were proud of their richness . . .

ARKËL.

I see there only a great innocence . . .

GOLAUD.

A great innocence! . . . They are greater than innocence! . . . They are purer than the eyes of a lamb . . . They would give God lessons in innocence! A great innocence! Listen: I am so near them I feel the freshness of their lashes when they wink; and yet I am less far away from the great secrets of the other world than from the smallest secret of those eyes! . . . A great innocence! . . . More than innocence! You would say the angels of heaven celebrated there an eternal baptism! . . . I know those eyes! I have seen them at their work! Close them! close them! or I shall close them for a long while! . . .—Do not put your right hand to your throat so; I am saying a very simple thing . . . I have no under-thought . . . If I had an under-thought, why should I not say it? Ah! ah!—do not attempt to flee!—Here!—Give me that hand!—Ah! your hands are too hot . . . Go away! Your flesh disgusts me! . . . Here!—There is no more question of fleeing now!—[*He seizes her by the hair.*]—You shall follow me on your knees!—On your knees!—On your knees before me!—Ah! ah! your long hair serves some purpose at last! . . . Right, . . . left!—Left, . . . right!—Absalom! Absalom.—Forward! back! To the ground! to the ground! . . . You see, you see; I laugh already like an old man . . .

ARKËL (running up).

Golaud! . . .

GOLAUD (affecting a sudden calm).

You will do as you may please, look you.—I attach no importance to that.—I am too old; and, besides, I am not a spy. I shall await chance; and then . . . Oh! then! . . . simply because it is the custom; simply because it is the custom . . . [*Exit.*

ARKËL.

What ails him?—He is drunk?

MÉLISANDE (in tears).

No, no; he does not love me any more . . . I am not happy! . . . I am not happy! . . .

ARKËL.

If I were God, I would have pity on men's hearts . . .

SCENE III.—*A terrace of the castle. Little* YNIOLD *discovered, trying to lift a bowlder.*

LITTLE YNIOLD.

Oh, this stone is heavy! . . . It is heavier than I am . . . It is heavier than everybody . . . It is heavier than everything that ever happened . . . I can see my golden ball between the rock and this naughty stone, and I cannot reach it . . . My little arm is not long enough, . . . and this stone won't be lifted . . . I can't lift it, . . . and nobody could lift it . . . It is heavier than the whole house; . . . you would think it had roots in the earth . . . [*The Bleatings of a flock heard far away.*]—Oh! oh! I hear the sheep crying . . . [*He goes to look, at the edge of the terrace.*] Why! there is no more sun . . . They are coming . . . the little sheep . . . they are coming . . . There is a lot of them! . . . There is a lot of them! . . . They are afraid of the dark . . . They crowd together! they crowd together! . . . They can hardly walk any more . . . They are crying! they are crying! and they go quick! . . . They go quick! . . . They are already at the great crossroads. Ah! ah! They don't know where they ought to go any more . . . They don't cry any more . . . They wait . . . Some of them want to go to the right . . . They all want to go to the right . . . They cannot! . . . The shepherd is throwing earth at them . . . Ah! ah! They are going to pass by here . . . They obey! They obey! They are going to pass under the terrace . . . They are going to pass under the rocks . . . I am going to see them near by . . . Oh! oh! what a lot of them! . . . What a lot of them! . . . The whole road is full of them . . . They all keep still now . . . Shepherd! shepherd! why don't they speak any more?

THE SHEPHERD (*who is out of sight*).

Because it is no longer the road to the stable . . .

YNIOLD.

Where are they going?—Shepherd! shepherd!—where are they going?—He doesn't hear me any more. They are too far away already . . . They go quick . . . They are not making a noise any more . . . It is no longer the road to the stable . . . Where are they going to sleep to-night?—Oh! oh!—It is too dark . . . I am going to tell something to somebody . . .

[*Exit.*

SCENE IV.—*A fountain in the park.*

Enter PÉLLÉAS.

PÉLLÉAS.

It is the last evening . . . the last evening. It must all end. I have played like a child about a thing I did not guess . . . I have played a-dream about the snares of fate . . . Who has awakened me all at once? I shall flee, crying out for joy and woe like a blind man fleeing from his burning house . . . I am going to tell her I shall flee . . . My father is out of danger; and I have no more reason to lie to myself . . . It is late; she does not come . . . I should do better to go away without seeing her again . . . I must look well at her this time . . . There are some things that I no longer recall . . . It seems at times as if I had not seen her for a hundred years . . . And I have not yet looked upon her look . . . There remains nought to me if I go away thus. And all those memories . . . it is as if I were to take away a little water in a muslin bag . . . I must see her one last time, to the bottom of her heart . . . I must tell her all that I have never told her.

Enter MÉLISANDE.

MÉLISANDE.

Pélléas!
Mélisande!—Is it thou, Mélisande?

MÉLISANDE.

Yes.

PÉLLÉAS.

Come hither; do not stay at the edge of the moonlight.—Come hither. We have so many things to tell each other . . . Come hither in the shadow of the linden.

MÉLISANDE.

Let me stay in the light . . .

PÉLLÉAS.

We might be seen from the windows of the tower. Come hither; here, we have nothing to fear.—Take care; we might be seen . . .

MÉLISANDE.

I wish to be seen . . .

PÉLLÉAS.

Why, what doth ail thee?—Thou wert able to come out without being seen?

MÉLISANDE.

Yes; your brother slept . . .

PÉLLÉAS.

It is late.—In an hour they will close the gates. We must be careful. Why art thou come so late?

MÉLISANDE.

Your brother had a bad dream. And then my gown was caught on the nails of the gate. See, it is torn. I lost all this time, and ran . . .

PÉLLÉAS.

My poor Mélisande! . . . I should almost be afraid to touch thee . . . Thou art still out of breath, like a hunted bird . . . It is for me, for me, thou doest all that? . . . I hear thy heart beat as if it were mine . . . Come hither . . . nearer, nearer me . . .

MÉLISANDE.

Why do you laugh?

PÉLLÉAS.

I do not laugh;—or else I laugh for joy, unwittingly . . . It were a weeping matter, rather . . .

MÉLISANDE.

We have come here before . . . I recollect . . .

PÉLLÉAS.

Yes . . . yes . . . Long months ago.—I knew not then . . . Knowest thou why I asked thee to come here to-night?

MÉLISANDE.

No.

PÉLLÉAS.

It is perhaps the last time I shall see thee ... I must go away
forever ...

MÉLISANDE.

Why sayest thou always thou wilt go away? ...

PÉLLÉAS.

I must tell thee what thou knowest already?—Thou knowest not what
I am going to tell thee?

MÉLISANDE.

Why, no; why, no; I know nothing—...

PÉLLÉAS.

Thou knowest not why I must go afar ... Thou knowest not it is
because ... [*He kisses her abruptly.*] I love thee ...

MÉLISANDE (in a low voice).

I love thee too ...

PÉLLÉAS.

Oh! oh! What saidst thou, Mélisande? ... I hardly heard it! ... Thou
sayest that in a voice coming from the end of the world! ... I hardly
heard thee ... Thou lovest me?—Thou lovest me too? ... Since
when lovest thou me? ...

MÉLISANDE.

Since always ... Since I saw thee ...

PÉLLÉAS.

Oh, how thou sayest that! . . . Thy voice seems to have blown across the sea in spring! . . . I have never heard it until now; . . . one would say it had rained on my heart! . . . Thou sayest that so frankly! . . . Like an angel questioned! . . . I cannot believe it, Mélisande! . . . Why shouldst thou love me?—Nay, why dost thou love me?—Is what thou sayest true?—Thou dost not mock me?—Thou dost not lie a little, to make me smile? . . .

MÉLISANDE.

No; I never lie; I lie but to thy brother . . .

PÉLLÉAS.

Oh, how thou sayest that! . . . Thy voice! thy voice! . . . It is cooler and more frank than the water is! . . . It is like pure water on my lips! . . . It is like pure water on my hands . . . Give me, give me thy hands! . . . Oh, how small thy hands are! . . . I did not know thou wert so beautiful! . . . I have never seen anything so beautiful before thee . . . I was fall of unrest; I sought throughout the house . . . I sought throughout the country . . . And I found not beauty . . . And now I have found thee! . . . I have found thee!.,. I do not think there could be on the earth a fairer woman! . . . Where art thou?—I no longer hear thee breathe . . .

MÉLISANDE.

Because I look on thee . . .

PÉLLÉAS.

Why dost thou look so gravely on me?—We are already in the shadow.—It is too dark under this tree. Come into the light. We cannot see how happy we are. Come, come; so little time remains to us . . .

MÉLISANDE.

No, no; let us stay here . . . I am nearer thee in the dark . . .

PÉLLÉAS.

Where are thine eyes?—Thou art not going to fly me?—Thou dost not think of me just now.

MÉLISANDE.

Oh, yes; oh, yes; I only think of thee . . .

PÉLLÉAS.

Thou wert looking elsewhere . . .

MÉLISANDE.

I saw thee elsewhere . . .

PÉLLÉAS.

Thy soul is far away . . . What ails thee, then?—Meseems thou art not happy . . .

MÉLISANDE.

Yes, yes; I am happy, but I am sad . . .

PÉLLÉAS.

One is sad often when one loves . . .

MÉLISANDE.

I weep always when I think of thee . . .

PÉLLÉAS.

I too . . . I too, Mélisande . . . I am quite near thee; I weep for joy, and yet . . . [He kisses her again.]—Thou art strange when I kiss thee so . . . Thou art so beautiful that one would think thou wert about to die . . .

MÉLISANDE.

Thou too . . .

PÉLLÉAS.

There, there . . . We do not what we will . . . I did not love thee the first time I saw thee . . .

MÉLISANDE.

Nor I . . . nor I . . . I was afraid . . .

PÉLLÉAS.

I could not admit thine eyes . . . I would have gone away at once . . . and then . . .

MÉLISANDE.

And I,—I would not have come . . . I do not yet know why,—I was afraid to come . . .

PÉLLÉAS.

There are so many things one never knows. We are ever waiting; and then . . . What is that noise?—They are closing the gates! . . .

MÉLISANDE.

Yes, they have closed the gates . . .

PÉLLÉAS.

We cannot go back now?—Hearest thou the bolts?—Listen! listen! . . . the great chains! . . . the great chains! . . . It is too late; it is too late! . . .

MÉLISANDE.

All the better! all the better! all the better! . . .

PÉLLÉAS.

Thou—. . . ? Behold, behold! . . . It is no longer we who will it so! . . . All's lost, all's saved! all is saved to-night!—Come, come . . . My heart beats like a madman,—up to my very throat . . . *[They embrace.]* Listen! listen! my heart is almost strangling me . . . Come! come! . . . Ah, how beautiful it is in the shadows! . . .

MÉLISANDE.

There is some one behind us! . . .

PÉLLÉAS.

I see no one . . .

MÉLISANDE.

I heard a noise . . .

PÉLLÉAS.

I hear only thy heart in the dark . . .

MÉLISANDE.

I heard the crackling of dead leaves . . .

PÉLLÉAS.

Because the wind is silent all at once . . . It fell as we were kissing . . .

MÉLISANDE.

How long our shadows are to-night! . . .

PÉLLÉAS.

They embrace to the very end of the garden. Oh, how they kiss far away from us! . . . Look! look! . . .

MÉLISANDE.(a stifled voice).

A-a-h!—He is behind a tree!

PÉLLÉAS.

Who?

MÉLISANDE.

Golaud!

PÉLLÉAS.

Golaud!—where?—I see nothing . . .

MÉLISANDE.

There . . . at the end of our shadows.

PÉLLÉAS.

Yes, yes; I saw him . . . Let us not turn abruptly . . .

MÉLISANDE.

He has his sword . . .

PÉLLÉAS.

I have not mine . . .

MÉLISANDE.

He saw us kiss . . .

PÉLLÉAS.

He does not know we have seen him . . . Do not stir; do not turn your head . . . He would rush headlong on us . . . He will remain there while he thinks we do not know. He watches us . . . He is still motionless . . . Go, go at once this way . . . I will wait for him . . . I will stop him . . .

MÉLISANDE.

No, no, no! . . .

PÉLLÉAS.

Go! go! he has seen all! . . . He will kill us! . . .

MÉLISANDE.

All the better! all the better! all the better! . . .

PÉLLÉAS.

He comes! he comes! . . . Thy mouth! . . . Thy mouth! . . .

MÉLISANDE.

Yes! . . . yes! yes! . . .
[They kiss desperately.

PÉLLÉAS

Oh! oh! All the stars are falling! . . .

MÉLISANDE.

Upon me too! upon me too! . . .

PÉLLÉAS.

Again! Again! . . . Give! give! . . .

MÉLISANDE.

All! all! all! . . .

[Golaud rushes upon them, sword in hand, and strikes Pélléas, who falls at the brink of the fountain. Mélisande flees terrified.]

MÉLISANDE. (fleeing).

Oh! oh! I have no courage I . . . I have no courage! . . .

[GOLAUD pursues her through the wood in silence.

ACT FIFTH.

SCENE I.—*A lower hall in the castle. The women servants discovered, gathered together, while without children are playing before one of the ventilators of the hall.*

AN OLD SERVANT.

You will see, you will see, my daughters; it will be to-night.—Some one will come to tell us by and by . . .

ANOTHER SERVANT.

They will not come to tell us . . . They don't know what they are doing any longer . . .

THIRD SERVANT.

Let us wait here . . .

FOURTH SERVANT.

We shall know well enough when we must go up . . .

FIFTH SERVANT.

When the time is come, we shall go up of ourselves . . .

SIXTH SERVANT.

There is no longer a sound heard in the house . . .

SEVENTH SERVANT.

We ought to make the children keep still, who are playing before the ventilator.

EIGHTH SERVANT.

They will be still of themselves by and by.

NINTH SERVANT.

The time has not yet come . . .

Enter an old Servant.

THE OLD SERVANT.

No one can go in the room any longer. I have listened more than an hour . . . You could hear the flies walk on the doors . . . I heard nothing . . .

FIRST SERVANT.

Has she been left alone in the room?

THE OLD SERVANT.

No, no; I think the room is full of people.

FIRST SERVANT.

They will come, they will come, by and by . . .

THE OLD SERVANT.

Lord! Lord! It is not happiness that has come into the house . . . One may not speak, but if I could say what I know . . .

SECOND SERVANT.

It was you who found them before the gate?

THE OLD SERVANT.

Why, yes! why, yes! it was I who found them. The porter says it was he who saw them first; but it was I who waked them. He was sleeping on his face and would not get up.—And now he comes saying, "It was I who saw them first." Is that just?—See, I burned myself lighting a lamp to go down cellar.—Now what was I going to do down cellar?— I can't remember any more what I was going to do down cellar.—At any rate I got up very early; it was not yet very light; I said to myself, I will go across the courtyard, and then I will open the gate. Good; I go down the stairs on tiptoe, and I open the gate as if it were an ordinary gate . . . My God! My God! What do I see? Divine a little what I see! . . .

FIRST SERVANT.

They were before the gate?

THE OLD SERVANT.

They were both stretched out before the gate! . . . Exactly like poor folk that are too hungry . . . They were huddled together like little children who are afraid . . . The little princess was nearly dead, and the great Golaud had still his sword in his side . . . There was blood on the sill . . .

SECOND SERVANT.

We ought to make the children keep still . . . They are screaming with all their might before the ventilator . . .

THIRD SERVANT.

You can't hear yourself speak . . .

FOURTH SERVANT.

There is nothing to be done: I have tried already; they won't keep still . . .

FIRST SERVANT.

It seems he is nearly cured?

THE OLD SERVANT.

Who?

FIRST SERVANT.

The great Golaud.

THIRD SERVANT.

Yes, yes; they have taken him to his wife's room. I met them just now, in the corridor. They were holding him up as if he were drunk. He cannot yet walk alone.

THE OLD SERVANT.

He could not kill himself; he is too big. But she is hardly wounded, and it is she who is going to die . . . Can you understand that?

FIRST SERVANT.

You have seen the wound?

THE OLD SERVANT.

As I see you, my daughter.—I saw everything, you understand . . . I saw it before all the others . . . A tiny little wound under her little left breast,—a little wound that wouldn't kill a pigeon. Is it natural?

FIRST SERVANT.

Yes, yes; there is something underneath . . .

SECOND SERVANT.

Yes; but she was delivered of her babe three days ago . . .

THE OLD SERVANT.

Exactly! . . . She was delivered on her death-bed; is that a little sign?— And what a child! Have you seen it?—A wee little girl a beggar would not bring into the world . . . A little wax figure that came much too soon; . . . a little wax figure that must live in lambs' wool . . . Yes, yes; it is not happiness that has come into the house . . .

FIRST SERVANT.

Yes, yes; it Is the hand of God that has been stirring . . .

SECOND SERVANT.

Yes, yes; all that did not happen without reason . . .

THIRD SERVANT.

It is as good lord Pélléas . . . where is he?—No one knows . . .

THE OLD SERVANT.

Yes, yes; everybody knows . . . But nobody dare speak of it . . . One does not speak of this; . . . one does not speak of that; . . . one speaks no more of anything; . . . one no longer speaks truth . . . But *I* know he was found at the bottom of Blind Man's Spring; . . . but no one, no one could see him . . . Well, well, we shall only know all that at the last day . . .

FIRST SERVANT.

I dare not sleep here any longer . . .

THE OLD SERVANT.

Yes, yes; once ill-fortune is in the house, one keeps silence in vain . . .

THIRD SERVANT.

Yes; it finds you all the same . . .

THE OLD SERVANT.

Yes, yes; but we do not go where we would . . .

FOURTH SERVANT.

Yes, yes; we do not do what we would . . .

FIRST SERVANT.

They are afraid of us now . . .

SECOND SERVANT.

They all keep silence . . .

THIRD SERVANT.

They cast down their eyes in the corridors.

FOURTH SERVANT.

They do not speak any more except in a low voice.

FIFTH SERVANT.

   You would think they had all done it together.

SIXTH SERVANT.

   One doesn't know what they have done . . .

SEVENTH SERVANT.

   What is to be done when the masters are afraid? . . . [*A silence.*

FIRST SERVANT.

   I no longer hear the children screaming.

SECOND SERVANT.

   They are sitting down before the ventilator.

THIRD SERVANT.

   They are huddled against each other.

THE OLD SERVANT.

   I no longer hear anything in the house . . .

FIRST SERVANT.

   You no longer even hear the children breathe . . .

THE OLD SERVANT.

   Come, come; it is time to go up . . .

   [*Exeunt in silence.*

SCENE II.—*An apartment in the castle.*

ARKËL, GOLAUD, and the PHYSICIAN discovered in one corner of the room. MÉLISANDE is stretched upon her bed.

THE PHYSICIAN.

It cannot be of that little wound she is dying; a bird would not have died of it . . . It is not you, then, who have killed her, good my lord; do not be so disconsolate . . . She could not have lived . . . She was born without reason . . . to die; and she dies without reason . . . And then, it is not sure we shall not save her . . .

ARKËL.

No, no; it seems to me we keep too silent, in spite of ourselves, in her room . . . It is not a good sign . . . Look how she sleeps . . . slowly, slowly; . . . it is as if her soul was cold forever . . .

GOLAUD.

I have killed her without cause! I have killed her without cause! . . . Is it not enough to make the stones weep? . . . They had kissed like little children . . . They had simply kissed . . . They were brother and sister . . . And I, and I at once! . . . I did it in spite of myself, look you . . . I did it in spite of myself . . .

THE PHYSICIAN.

Stop; I think she is waking . . .

MÉLISANDE.

Open the window; . . . open the window . . .

ARKËL

Shall I open this one, Mélisande?

MÉLISANDE.

No, no; the great window . . . the great window . . . It is to see . . .

ARKËL.

Is not the sea air too cold to-night? Do it; do it . . .

MÉLISANDE.

Thanks . . . Is it sunset?

ARKËL.

Yes; it is sunset on the sea; it is late.—How are you, Mélisande?

MÉLISANDE.

Well, well.—Why do you ask that? I have never been better.—And yet it seems to me I know something . . .

ARKËL.

What sayest thou?—I do not understand thee . . .

MÉLISANDE.

Neither do I understand all I say, you see . . . I do not know what I am saying . . . I do not know what I know . . . I no longer say what I would . . .

ARKËL.

Why, yes! why, yes! . . . I am quite happy to hear thee speak so; thou hast raved a little these last days, and one no longer understood thee . . . But now all that is far away . . .

MÉLISANDE.

I do not know . . .—Are you all alone in the room, grandfather?

ARKËL.

No; there is the physician, besides, who cured thee . . .

MÉLISANDE.

Ah! . . .

ARKËL.

And then there is still some one else . . .

MÉLISANDE.

Who is it?

ARKËL.

It is . . . thou must not be frightened . . . He does not wish thee the least harm, be sure . . . If thou'rt afraid, he will go away . . . He is very unhappy . . .

MÉLISANDE.

Who is it?

ARKËL.

It is thy . . . thy husband . . . It is Golaud . . .

MÉLISANDE.

Golaud is here? Why does he not come by me?

GOLAUD (dragging himself toward the bed.)
Mélisande . . . Mélisande . . .

MÉLISANDE.

Is it you, Golaud? I should hardly recognize you any more . . . It is the evening sunlight in my eyes . . . Why look you on the walls? You have grown thin and old . . . Is it a long while since we saw each other?

GOLAUD (to ARKËL and the PHYSICIAN).

Will you withdraw a moment, if you please, if you please? . . . I will leave the door wide open . . . One moment only . . . I would say something to her; else I could not die . . . Will you?—Go clear to the end of the corridor; you can come back at once, at once . . . Do not refuse me this . . . I am a wretch . . . [*Exit ARKËL and the PHYSICIAN.*]—Mélisande, hast thou pity on me, as I have pity on thee? . . . Mélisande? . . . Dost thou forgive me, Mélisande? . . .

MÉLISANDE.

Yes, yes, I do forgive thee . . . What must I forgive? . . .

GOLAUD.

I have wrought thee so much ill, Mélisande . . . I cannot tell thee the ill I have wrought thee . . . But I see it, I see it so clearly to-day . . . since the first day . . . And all I did not know till now leaps in my eyes to-night . . . And it is all my fault, all that has happened, all that will happen . . . If I could tell it, thou wouldst see as I do! . . . I see all! I see all! . . . But I loved thee so! . . . I loved thee so! . . . But now there is some one dying . . . It is I who am dying . . . And I would know . . . I would ask thee . . . Thou'lt bear me no ill-will . . . I would . . . The truth must be told to a dying man . . . He must know the truth, or else he could not sleep . . . Swearest thou to tell me the truth?

MÉLISANDE

Yes.

GOLAUD.

Didst thou love Pélléas?

MÉLISANDE.

Why, yes; I loved him.—Where is he?

GOLAUD.

Thou dost not understand me?—Thou wilt not understand me?—It seems to me ... it seems to me ... Well, then, here: I ask thee if thou lovedst him with a forbidden love? ... Wert thou ... were you guilty? Say, say, yes, yes, yes! ...

MÉLISANDE.

No, no; we were not guilty.—Why do you ask that?

GOLAUD.

Mélisande! ... tell me the truth, for the love of God!

MÉLISANDE.

Why have I not told the truth?

GOLAUD.

Do not lie so any more, at the moment of death!

MÉLISANDE.

Who is dying?—Is it I?

GOLAUD.

Thou, thou! and I, I too, after thee! ... And we must have the truth ... We must have the truth at last, dost thou understand? ... Tell me all! Tell me all! I forgive thee all! ...

MÉLISANDE.

Why am I going to die?—I did not know it . . .

GOLAUD.

Thou knowest it now! . . . It is time! It is time! . . . Quick! quick! . . . The truth! the truth! . . .

MÉLISANDE.

The truth . . . the truth . . .

GOLAUD.

Where art thou?—Mélisande!—Where art thou?—It is not natural! Mélisande! Where art thou?—Where goest thou? [*Perceiving ARKËL and the PHYSICIAN at the door of the room.*]— Yes, yes; you may come in . . . I know nothing; it is useless . . . It is too late; she is already too far away from us . . . I shall never know! . . . I shall die here like a blind man! . . .

ARKËL.

What have you done? You will kill her . . .

GOLAUD.

I have already killed her . . .

ARKËL.

Mélisande . . .

MÉLISANDE.

Is it you, grandfather?

ARKËL.

Yes, my daughter . . . What would you have me do?

MÉLISANDE.

Is it true that the winter is beginning? . . .

ARKËL.

Why dost thou ask?

MÉLISANDE.

Because it is cold, and there are no more leaves . . .

ARKËL.

Thou art cold?—Wilt thou have the windows closed?

MÉLISANDE.

No, no, . . . not till the sun be at the bottom of the sea.—It sinks slowly; then it is the winter beginning?

ARKËL.

Yes.—Thou dost not like the winter?

MÉLISANDE.

Oh! no. I am afraid of the cold.—I am so afraid of the great cold . . .

ARKËL.

Dost thou feel better?

MÉLISANDE.

Yes, yes; I have no longer all those qualms . . .

ARKËL.

Wouldst thou see thy child?

MÉLISANDE.

What child?

ARKËL.

Thy child.—Thou art a mother . . . Thou hast brought a little daughter
into the world . . .

MÉLISANDE.

Where is she?

ARKËL.

Here . . .

MÉLISANDE.

It is strange . . . I cannot lift my arms to take her . . .

ARKËL.

Because you are still very weak . . . I will hold her myself; look . . .

MÉLISANDE.

She does not laugh . . . She is little . . . She is going to weep too . . . I
pity her . . .
[The room has been invaded, little by little, by the women
servants of the castle, who range themselves in silence along
the walls and wait]

GOLAUD (rising abruptly).

What is the matter?—What are all these women coming here
for? . . .

THE PHYSICIAN.

It is the servants . . .

ARKËL.

Who was it called them?

THE PHYSICIAN.

It was not I . . .

GOLAUD.

Why do you come here?—No one has asked for you . . . What come you here to do?—But what is it, then?—Answer me! . . .
[The servants make no answer.

ARKËL.

Do not speak too loud . . . She is going to sleep; she has closed her eyes . . .

GOLAUD.

It is not . . . ?

THE PHYSICIAN.

No, no; see, she breathes . . .

ARKËL.

Her eyes are full of tears.—It is her soul weeping now . . . Why does she stretch her arms out so?—What would she?

THE PHYSICIAN.

It is toward the child, without doubt . . . It is the straggle of motherhood against . . .

GOLAUD.

At this moment?—At this moment?—You must say. Say! Say! . . .

THE PHYSICIAN.

Perhaps.

GOLAUD.

At once? . . . Oh! oh! I must tell her . . .—Mélisande! Mélisande! . . . Leave me alone! leave me alone with her! . . .

ARKËL.

No, no; do not come near . . . Trouble her not . . . Speak no more to her . . . You know not what the soul is . . .

GOLAUD.

It is not my fault! . . . It is not my fault!

ARKËL.

Hush! . . . Hush! . . . We must speak softly now.—She must not be disturbed . . . The human soul is very silent . . . The human soul likes to depart alone . . . It suffers so timorously . . . But the sadness, Golaud . . . the sadness of all we see! . . . Oh! oh! oh! . . . [At this moment, all the servants fall suddenly on their knees at the back of the chamber.]

ARKËL (turning).

What is the matter?

THE PHYSICIAN (approaching the bed and feeling the body).

They are right . . .
[A long silence.

ARKËL.

I saw nothing.—Are you sure? . . .

THE PHYSICIAN.

Yes, yes.

ARKËL.

I heard nothing . . . So quick, so quick! . . . All at once! . . . She goes without a word . . .

GOLAUD (sobbing).

Oh! oh! oh!

ARKËL.

Do not stay here, Golaud . . . She must have silence now . . . Come, come . . . It is terrible, but it is not your fault . . . 'T was a little being, so quiet, so fearful, and so silent . . . 'T was a poor little mysterious being, like everybody . . . She lies there as if she were the big sister of her child . . . Come, come . . . My God! My God! . . . I shall never understand it at all . . . Let us not stay here.—Come; the child most not stay here in this room . . . She must live now in her place . . . It is the poor little one's turn . . .

[They go out in silence.

[CURTAIN.]

ALLADINE AND PALOMIDES.

To Camille Mauclair.

PERSONS.

ABLAMORE.

ASTOLAINE, *daughter of Ablamore.*

ALLADINE.

PALOMIDES.

THE SISTERS OF PALOMIDES.

A PHYSICIAN.

[NOTE: The translation of Ablamore's song is taken from the version of this play made by the editors of "Poet-lore." R.H.]

ACT FIRST.

A-wild part of the gardens. ABLAMORE discovered leaning over ALLADINE, who is asleep.

ABLAMORE.

Methinks sleep reigns day and night beneath these trees. Each time she comes here with me toward nightfall, she is hardly seated when she falls asleep. Alas! I must be glad even of that . . . During the day, whene'er I speak to her and her look happens to encounter mine, it is hard as a slave's to whom a thing impossible has just been bidden . . . Yet that is not her customary look . . . I have seen her many times resting her beautiful eyes on children, on the forest, the sea, or her surroundings. She smiles at me as one smiles on a foe; and I dare not bend over her save at times when her eyes can no longer see me . . . I have a few moments every evening; and all the rest of the day I live beside her with my eyes cast down . . . It is sad to love too late . . . Maids cannot understand that years do not separate hearts . . . They have called me "The wise King." . . . I was wise because till now nothing had happened to me . . . There are men who seem to turn events aside. It was enough that I should be about for nothing to be able to have birth . . . I had suspected it of old . . . In the time of my youth, I had many friends whose presence seemed to attract every adventure; but the days when I went forth with them, for the encounter of joys or sorrows, they came back again with empty hands . . . I think I palsied fate; and I long took pride in this gift. One lived under cover in my reign . . . But now I have recognized that misfortune itself is better worth than sleep, and that there must be a life more active and higher than waiting . . . They shall see that I too have strength to trouble, when I will, the water that seems dead at the bottom of the great caldrons of the future . . . Alladine, Alladine! . . . Oh! she is lovely so, her hair over the flowers and over her pet lamb, her lips apart and fresher than the morn . . . I will kiss her without her knowing, holding back my poor white beard . . . *[He kisses her.]*—She smiled . . . Should I pity her? For the few years she gives me, she will some day be queen; and I shall have done a little good before I go away . . . They will be astonished . . . She herself does not know . . . Ah! here she wakes with a start . . . Where are you coming from, Alladine?

ALLADINE.

I have had a bad dream . . .

ABLAMORE.

What is the matter? Why do you look yonder?

ALLADINE.

Some one went by upon the road.

ABLAMORE.

I heard nothing.

ALLADINE.

I tell you some one is coming . . . There he is! [*She points out a young knight coming forward through the trees and holding his horse by the bridle.*] Do not take me by the hand; I am not afraid . . . He has not seen us . . .

ABLAMORE.

Who dares come here? . . . If I did not know . . . I believe it is Palomides . . . It is Astolaine's betrothed . . . He has raised his head . . . Is it you, Palomides?

Enter PALOMIDES.

PALOMIDES.

Yes, my father . . . If I am suffered yet to call you by that name . . . I come hither before the day and the hour . . .

ABLAMORE.

You are a welcome guest, whatever hour it be . . . But what has happened? We did not expect you for two days yet . . . Is Astolaine here, too? . . .

PALOMIDES.

No; she will come to-morrow. We have journeyed day and night. She was tired and begged me to come on before . . . Are my sisters come?

ABLAMORE.

They have been here three days waiting for your wedding.——You look very happy, Palomides . . .

PALOMIDES.

Who would not be happy, to have found what he sought? I was sad of old. But now the days seem lighter and more sweet than harmless birds in the hand . . . And if old moments come again by chance, I draw near Astolaine, and you would think I threw a window open on the dawn . . . She has a soul that can be seen around her,——that takes you in its arms like an ailing child and without saying anything to you consoles you for everything . . . I shall never understand it at all.——I do not know how it can all be; but my knees bend in spite of me when I speak of it . . .

ALLADINE.

I want to go in again.

ABLAMORE.

[Seeing that ALLADINE and PALOMIDES look at each other stealthily.] This is little Alladine who has come hither from the heart of Arcady . . . Take hands . . . Does that astonish you, Palomides? . . .

PALOMIDES.

My father . . .

[PALOMIDES' horse starts aside, frightening ALLADINE'S lamb.]

116

ABLAMORE.

Take care . . . Your horse has frightened Alladine's lamb . . . He will run away . . .

ALLADINE.

No; he never runs away . . . He has been startled, but he will not run away . . . It is a lamb my godmother gave me . . . He is not like others . . . He stays beside me night and day. *[Caressing it.*

PALOMIDES (also caressing it).

He looks at me with the eyes of a child . . .

ALLADINE.

He understands everything that happens . . .

ABLAMORE.

It is time to go find your sisters, Palomides . . . They will be astonished to see you . . .

ALLADINE.

They have gone every day to the turning of the road . . . I have gone with them; but they did not hope yet . . .

ABLAMORE.

Come; Palomides is covered with dust, and he must be weary . . . We have too many things to say to each other to talk here . . . We will say them to-morrow . . . They claim the morn is wiser than the evening . . . I see the palace gates are open and seem to wait for us . . .

ALLADINE.

I cannot help being uneasy when I go back into the palace . . . It is so big, and I am so little, and I get lost there still . . . And then all those windows on the sea . . . You cannot count them . . . And the corridors that turn without reason, and others that never turn, but lose themselves between the walls . . . And the halls I dare not go into . . .

PALOMIDES.

We will go in everywhere . . .

ALLADINE.

You would think I was not made to dwell there,—that it was not built for me . . . Once I lost my way there . . . I pushed open thirty doors, before I found the light of day again . . . And I could not go out; the last door opened on a pool . . . And the vaults that are cold all summer; and the galleries that bend back on themselves endlessly . . . There are stairways that lead nowhere and terraces from which nothing can be seen . . .

ABLAMORE.

You who were not wont to talk, how you talk to-night! . . .

[Exeunt.

ACT SECOND.

SCENE I.—ALLADINE discovered, her forehead against one of the windows that open on the park. Enter ABLAMORE.

ABLAMORE.

Alladine . . .

ALLADINE (turning abruptly).

   What is it?

ABLAMORE.

   Oh, how pale you are! . . . Are you ill?

ALLADINE.

   No.

ABLAMORE.

   What is it in the park?—Were you looking at the avenue of fountains that unfolds before your windows?—They are wonderful and weariless. They were raised there one by one, at the death of each of my daughters . . . At night I hear them singing in the garden . . . They bring to mind the lives they represent, and I can tell their voices apart . . .

ALLADINE.

   I know.

ABLAMORE.

   You must pardon me; I sometimes repeat the same things and my memory is less trust-worthy . . . It is not age; I am not an old man yet, thank God! but kings have a thousand cares. Palomides has been telling me his adventures . . .

ALLADINE.

   Ah!

ABLAMORE.

   He has not done what he would; young people have no will any more.—He astonishes me. I had chosen him among a thousand for

119

my daughter. He should have had a soul as deep as hers.——He has done nothing which may not be excusable, but I had hoped more . . . What do you say of him?

ALLADINE.

Who?

ABLAMORE.

Palomides?

ALLADINE.

I have only seen him one evening . . .

ABLAMORE.

He astonishes me.——Everything has succeeded with him till now. He would undertake a thing and accomplish it without a word.—— He would get out of danger without an effort, while others could not open a door without finding death behind it.——He was of those whom events seem to await on their knees. But a little while ago something snapped. You would say he has no longer the same star, and every step he takes carries him further from himself.——I don't know what it is.——He does not seem to be at all aware, but others can remark it . . . Let us speak of something else: look! the night comes; I see it rise along the walls. Would you like to go together to the wood of Astolat, as we do other evenings?

ALLADINE.

I am not going out to-night.

ABLAMORE.

We will stay here, since you prefer it so. Yet the air is sweet and the evening very fair. [*ALLADINE starts without his noticing it.*] I have had flowers set along the hedges, and I should like to show them to you . . .

ALLADINE.

No, not to-night . . . If you wish me to . . . I like to go there with you . . . the air is pure and the trees . . . but not to-night . . . [*Cowers, weeping, against the old man's breast.*] I do not feel quite well . . .

ABLAMORE.

What is the matter? You are going to fall . . . I will call . . .

ALLADINE.

No, no . . . It is nothing . . . It is over . . .

ABLAMORE.

Sit down. Wait . . .

[*He runs to the folding-doors at the back and opens both. Palomides is seen, seated on a bench. He has not had time to turn away his eyes. Ablamore looks fixedly at him, without a word, then re-enters the room. Palomides rises and retreats in the corridor, stifling the sound of his footsteps. The pet lamb leaves the room, unperceived.*]

SCENE II.—A drawbridge over the moats of the palace. PALOMIDES and ALLADINE, with her pet lamb, appear at the two ends of the bridge. KING ABLAMORE leans out from a window of the tower.

PALOMIDES.

Were you going out, Alladine?—I was coming in. I am coming back from the chase.—It rained.

ALLADINE.

I have never passed this bridge.

PALOMIDES.

It leads to the forest. It is seldom passed. People had rather go a long way around. I think they are afraid because the moats are deeper at this place than elsewhere, and the black water that comes down from the mountains boils horribly between the walls before it goes hurling itself into the sea. It roars there always; but the quays are so high you hardly notice it. It is the most deserted wing of the palace. But on this side the forest is more beautiful, more ancient, and greater than any you have seen. It is full of unusual trees and flowers that have sprung up of themselves,—Will you come?

ALLADINE.

I do not know . . . I am afraid of the roaring water.

PALOMIDES.

Come, come; it roars without reason. Look at your lamb; he looks at me as if he wished to come . . . Come, come . . .

ALLADINE.

Don't call him . . . He will get away.

PALOMIDES.

Come, come.
[The lamb escapes from Alladine's hands, and comes leaping toward Palomides, but slips on the inclined plane of the drawbridge and goes rolling into the moat.]

ALLADINE.

What has he done?—Where is he?

PALOMIDES.

He slipped. He is straggling in the heart of the eddy. Do not look at him; there is nothing to be done . . .

ALLADINE.

You are going to save him?

PALOMIDES.

Save him? But look! he is already in the tunnel. One moment more, and he will be under the vaults; and God himself will never see him more . . .

ALLADINE.

Go away! Go away!

PALOMIDES.

What is the matter?

ALLADINE.

Go away!—I do not want to see you any more! . . .

[Ablamore enters precipitately, seizes Alladine, and draws her away brusquely without speaking.]

SCENE III.—A room in the palace. ABLAMORE and ALLADINE discovered.

ABLAMORE.

You see, Alladine, my hands do not tremble, my heart beats like a sleeping child's, and my voice has not once been stirred with wrath. I bear no ill-will to Palomides, although what he has done might seem unpardonable. And as for thee, who could bear thee ill-will? You obey

123

laws you do not know, and you could not act otherwise, I will not speak to you of what took place the other day along the palace moats, nor of all the unforeseen death of the lamb might have revealed to me, had I believed in omens for an instant. But last night I surprised the kiss you gave each other under the windows of Astolaine. At that moment I was with her in her room. She has a soul that fears so much to trouble, with a tear or with a simple movement of her eyelids, the happiness of those about her, that I shall never know if she, as I, surprised that wretched kiss. But I know what she has the power to suffer. I shall not ask you anything you cannot avow to me, but I would know if you had any secret design in following Palomides under the window where you must have seen us. Answer me without fear; you know beforehand I will pardon everything.

ALLADINE.
I did not kiss him.

ABLAMORE.
What? You did not kiss Palomides, and Palomides did not kiss you?

ALLADINE.
No.

ABLAMORE.
Ah! . . . Listen: I came here to forgive you everything . . . I thought you had acted as we almost all act, without aught of our soul intervening . . . But now I will know all that passed . . . You love Palomides, and you have kissed him under my eyes . . .

ALLADINE.
No.

ABLAMORE.

Don't go away. I am only an old man. Do not flee . . .

ALLADINE.

I am not fleeing.

ABLAMORE.

Ah! ah! You do not flee, because you think my old hands harmless! They have yet the strength to tear a secret out in spite of all *[He seizes her arms.*] And they could wrestle with all those you prefer . . . *[He twists her arms behind her head.*] Ah! you will not speak! . . . There will yet come a time when all your soul shall spirt out like a clear spring, for woe . . .

ALLADINE.

No, no!

ABLAMORE.

Again, . . . we are not at the end, the journey is very long—and naked truth is hid among the rocks . . . Will she come forth? . . . I see her gestures in your eyes already, and her cool breath will lave my visage soon . . . Ah! . . . Alladine! Alladine! . . . *[He releases her suddenly.*] I heard your bones cry out like little children . . . I have not hurt you? . . . Do not stay thus, upon your knees before me, . . . It is I who go down on my knees. *[He does as he says*] I am a wretch . . . You must have pity . . . It is not for myself alone I pray . . . I have only one poor daughter . . . All the rest are dead . . . I had seven of them about me . . . They were fair and full of happiness; and I saw them no more . . . The only one left to me is going to die, too . . . She did not love life . . . But one day she encountered something she no longer looked for, and I saw she had lost the desire to die . . . I do not ask a thing impossible . . . *[ALLADINE weeps and makes no answer.*]

SCENE IV.—The apartment of ASTOLAINE. ASTOLAINE and PALOMIDES discovered.

PALOMIDES.

Astolaine, when I met you several months ago by chance, it seemed to me that I had found at last what I had sought for during many years . . . Till you, I did not know all that the ever tenderer goodness and complete simplicity of a high soul might be. I was so deeply stirred by it that it seemed to me the first time I had met a human being. You would have said that I had lived till then in a closed chamber which you opened for me; and all at once I knew what must be the soul of other men and what mine might become . . . Since then, I have known you further. I have seen you act, and others too have taught me all that you have been.

There have been evenings when I quitted you without a word, and went to weep for wonder in a corner of the palace, because you had simply raised your eyes, made a little unconscious gesture, or smiled for no apparent cause, yet at the moment when all the souls about you asked it and would be satisfied. There is but you who know these moments, because you are, it seems, the soul of all, and I do not believe those who have not drawn near you can know what true life is. To-day I come to say all this to you, because I feel that I shall never be he whom I hoped once to become . . . A chance has come—or haply I myself have come; for you can never tell if you have made a movement of yourself, or if it be chance that has met with you—a chance has come, which has opened my eyes, just as we were about to make each other unhappy; and I have recognized there must be something more incomprehensible than the beauty of the most beautiful soul or the most beautiful face; and mightier, too, since I must needs obey it . . . I do not know if you have understood me. If you understand, have pity on me . . . I have said to myself all that could be said . . . I know what I shall lose, for I know her soul is a child's soul, a poor strengthless child's, beside yours, and yet I cannot resist it . . .

ASTOLAINE.

Do not weep . . . I know too that one does not do what one would do . . . nor was I ignorant that you would come . . . There must indeed be laws mightier than those of our souls, of which we always speak . . . *[Kissing him abruptly]*.—But I love thee the more, my poor Palomides.

PALOMIDES.

I love thee, too . . . more than her I love . . . Thou weepest, as I do?

ASTOLAINE.

They are little tears . . . Do not be sad for them . . . I weep so, because I am woman, but they say our tears are not painful . . . You see I can dry them already . . . I knew well what it was . . . I waited for the wakening . . . It has come, and I can breathe with less disquietude, being no longer happy . . . There! . . . We must see clearly now for you and her. For I believe my father already has suspicions. *[Exeunt.*

ACT THIRD.

SCENE I.—A room in the palace. ABLAMORE discovered. ASTOLAINE stands on the step of a half-open door at the back of the hall.

ASTOLAINE.

Father, I have come because a voice that I no longer can resist, commands me to. I told you all that happened in my soul when I met Palomides. He was not like other men . . . To-day I come to ask your help . . . for I do not know what should be said to him . . . I have become aware I cannot love him . . . He has remained the same, and I alone have changed, or have not understood . . . And since it is impossible for me to love, as I have dreamed of love, him I had chosen among all, it must be that my heart is shut to these things . . . I know it to-day . . . I shall look no more toward love; and you will see me living on about you without sadness and without unrest . . . I feel that I am going to be happy . . .

ABLAMORE.

Come hither, Astolaine. It is not so that you were wont to speak in the old days to your father. You wait there, on the threshold of a door hardly ajar, as if you were ready to flee; and with your hand upon the key, as if you would close from me forever the secret of your heart. You know quite well I have not understood what you have just said, and that words have no sense when souls are not within reach of each other. Draw nearer still, and speak no more to me, [*ASTOLAINE approaches slowly.*] There is a moment when souls touch each other, and know all without need that one should move the lips. Draw nearer . . . They do not reach each other yet, and their radiance is so slight about us! . . . [*ASTOLAINE stops.*] Thou darest not?—Thou knowest too how far one can go?—It is I who must . . . [*He approaches Astolaine with slow step, then stops and looks long at her.*] I see thee, Astolaine . . .

ASTOLAINE.

Father! . . . [*She sobs as she kisses the old man.*]

ABLAMORE.

You see well it was useless . . .

SCENE II.—*A chamber in the palace.*

Enter ALLADINE and PALOMIDES.

PALOMIDES.

All will be ready to-morrow. We cannot wait longer. He prowls like a madman through the corridors of the palace; I met him even now. He looked at me without a word. I passed; and as I turned, I saw him slyly laugh, shaking his keys. When he perceived that I was looking at him, he smiled at me, making signs of friendship. He must have some secret project, and we are in the hands of a master whose reason begins to totter . . . To-morrow we shall be far away . . . Yonder there are wonderful countries that resemble thine . . . Astolaine has already provided for our flight and for my sisters' . . .

ALLADINE.

What has she said?

PALOMIDES.

Nothing, nothing . . . You will see everything about my father's castle,—after days of sea and days of forests—you will see lakes and mountains . . . not like these, under a sky that looks like the vault of a cave, with black trees that the storms destroy . . . but a sky beneath which there is nothing more to fear,—forests that are always awake, flowers that do not close . . .

ALLADINE.

She wept?

PALOMIDES.

What are you asking? . . . There is something there of which we have no right to speak, do you understand? . . . There is a life there that does not belong to our poor life, and which love has no right to approach except in silence . . . We are here, like two beggars in rags, when I think of it . . . Go! go! . . . I could tell you things . . .

ALLADINE.

Palomides! . . . What is the matter?

PALOMIDES.

Go! go! . . . I have seen tears that came from further than the eyes . . . There is something else . . . It may be, nevertheless, that we are right . . . but how I regret being right so, my God! . . . Go! . . . I will tell you to-morrow . . . to-morrow . . . to-morrow . . .

[*Exeunt severally.*

SCENE III.—A corridor before the apartment of ALLADINE. Enter ASTOLAINE and the SISTERS OF PALOMIDES.

ASTOLAINE.

The horses wait in the forest, but Palomides will not flee; and yet your lives and his are in danger. I do not know my poor father any longer. He has a fixed idea that troubles his reason. This is the third day I have followed him step by step, hiding myself behind the pillars and the walls, for he suffers no one to companion him. To-day, as the other days, and from the first gleams of the morning he has gone wandering through the corridors and halls of the palace, and along the moats and ramparts, shaking the great golden keys he has had made and singing at the top of his voice the strange song whose refrain, *Go follow what your eyes have seen*, has perhaps pierced even to the depths of your chambers. I have concealed from you till now all that has come to pass, because such things must not be spoken of without reason. He must have shut up Alladine in this apartment, but no one knows what he has done with her. I have listened at the doors every night and whenever he has been away a moment, but I have never heard any noise in the room . . . Do you hear anything?

ONE OF THE SISTERS OF PALOMIDES.

No; I hear only the murmur of the air passing through the little chinks of the wood . . .

ANOTHER SISTER.

It seems to me, when I listen hard, that I hear the great pendulum of the clock.

A THIRD SISTER.

But what is this little Alladine, then, and why does he bear such ill-will to her?

ASTOLAINE.

It is a little Greek slave that came from the heart of Arcady . . . He bears her no ill-will, but . . . Do you hear?—It is my father . . . [*Singing heard in the distance.*] Hide yourselves behind the pillars . . . He will have no one pass by this corridor.—[*They hide.*]
Enter ABLAMORE, singing and shaking a bunch of great keys.

ABLAMORE (sings).

Misfortune had three golden keys.
—He has no rescue for the Queen!—
Misfortune had three golden keys.
Go follow what your eyes have seen.
[*Sits dejected on a bench, beside the door of Alladine's apartment, hums a little while longer, and soon goes to sleep, his arms hanging down and his head fallen.*]

ASTOLAINE.

Come, come! make no noise. He has fallen asleep on the bench.—Oh, my poor old father! How white his hair has grown during these days! He is so weak, he is so unhappy, that sleep itself no longer brings him peace. It is three whole days now since I have dared to look upon his face . . .

ONE OF THE SISTERS OF PALOMIDES.

He sleeps profoundly . . .

ASTOLAINE.

He sleeps profoundly, but you can see his soul has no rest . . . The sunlight here will vex his eyelids . . . I am going to draw his cloak over his face . . .

ANOTHER SISTER.

No, no; do not touch it . . . He might wake with a start . . .

ASTOLAINE.

Some one is coming in the corridor. Come, come! put yourselves before him . . . Hide him . . . A stranger must not see him in this state . . .

A SISTER OF PALOMIDES.

It is Palomides . . .

ASTOLAINE.

I am going to cover his poor eyes . . . [*She covers ABLAMORE'S face.*]— I would not have Palomides see him thus . . . He is too miserable.

Enter PALOMIDES.

PALOMIDES.

What is the matter?

ONE OF THE SISTERS.

He has fallen asleep on the bench.

PALOMIDES.

I have followed him without his seeing me . . . He said nothing? . . .

ASTOLAINE.

No; but see all he has suffered . . .

PALOMIDES.

Has he the keys?

ANOTHER SISTER.

He holds them in his hand . . .

PALOMIDES.

I am going to take them.

ASTOLAINE.

What are you going to do? Oh, do not wake him! . . . For three nights now he has wandered through the palace . . .

PALOMIDES.

I will open his hand a little without his noticing it . . . We have no right to wait any longer . . . God knows what he has done . . . He will forgive us when he has his reason back . . . Oh! oh! his hand has no strength any more . . .

ASTOLAINE.

Take care! Take care!

PALOMIDES.

I have the keys.—Which is it? I am going to open the room.

ONE OF THE SISTERS.

Oh, I am afraid! . . . Do not open it at once . . . Palomides! . . .

PALOMIDES.

Stay here . . . I do not know what I shall find . . .

[He goes to the door, opens it, and enters the apartment.]

ASTOLAINE.

Is she there?

PALOMIDES (in the apartment).

I cannot see . . . The shutters are closed . . .

ASTOLAINE.

Have a care, Palomides . . . Wilt thou that I go first? . . . Thy voice is trembling . . .

PALOMIDES (in the apartment).

No, no . . . I see a ray of sunlight falling through the chinks of the shutters.

ONE OF THE SISTERS.

Yes; it is broad day out of doors.

PALOMIDES.

[*Rushing headlong from the room.*] Come! Come! . . . I think she . . .

ASTOLAINE.

Thou hast seen her? . . .

PALOMIDES.

She is stretched out on the bed! . . . She does not stir! . . . I do not think she . . . Come! Come! [*They all go into the room.*

ASTOLAINE AND THE SISTERS OF PALOMIDES.

[*In the room.*] She is here . . . No, no, she is not dead . . . Alladine! Alladine! . . . Oh! oh! The poor child! . . . Do not cry out so . . . She has fainted . . . Her hair is tied across her mouth . . . And her hands are bound behind her back . . . They are bound with the help of her hair . . . Alladine! Alladine! . . . Fetch some water . . .

[ABLAMORE, who has waked, appears on the step of the door.]

ASTOLAINE.

There is my father! . . .

ABLAMORE (going to PALOMIDES).

Was it you who opened the door of the room?

PALOMIDES.

Yes, it was I . . . I did it—well, then?—well, then? . . . I could not let her die under my eyes . . . See what you have done. Alladine! . . . Fear nothing . . . She opens her eyes a little . . . I will not . . .

ABLAMORE.

Do not cry out . . . Do not cry out so . . . Come, we will open the shutters . . . You cannot see here. Alladine! . . . She is already sitting up. Alladine, come too . . . Do you see, my children, it is dark in the room. It is as dark here as if we were a thousand feet under the ground. But I open one of the shutters, and behold! All the light of the sky and the sun! . . . It does not need much effort; the light is full of good-will . . . It suffices that one call it; it always obeys . . . Have you seen the river with its little islands between the meadows in flower? . . . The sky is a crystal ring to-day . . . Alladine! Palomides, come see . . . Draw both of you near Paradise . . . You must kiss each other in the new light . . . I bear you no ill-will. You did what was ordained; and so did I . . . Lean out a moment from the open window, and look once more at the sweet green things . . .

[*A silence. He closes the shutter without a word.*]

ACT FOURTH.

Vast subterranean crypts. ALLADINE and PALOMIDES.

PALOMIDES.

They have bound my eyes with bands; they have tied my hands with cords.

ALLADINE.

They have tied my hands with cords; they have bound my eyes with bands . . . I think my hands are bleeding . . .

PALOMIDES.

Wait. To-day I bless my strength . . . I feel the knots beginning to give way . . . One struggle more, and let my fists burst! One struggle more! I have my hands! [*Tearing away the bandage.*] And my eyes! . . .

ALLADINE.

You see now?

PALOMIDES.

Yes.

ALLADINE.

Where are we?

PALOMIDES.

Where are you?

ALLADINE.

Here; can you not see me?

PALOMIDES.

My eyes weep still where the band has left its trace . . . We are not in darkness . . . Is it you I hear toward where I can just see?

ALLADINE.

I am here; come.

PALOMIDES.

You are at the edge of that which gives us light. Do not stir; I cannot see all that there is about you. My eyes have not forgot the bandage yet. They bound it tight enough to burst my eyelids.

ALLADINE.

Come; the knots stifle me. I can wait no longer . . .

PALOMIDES.

I hear only a voice coming out of the light . . .

ALLADINE.

Where are you?

PALOMIDES.

I have no idea myself. I walk still in darkness . . . Speak again, that I may find you. You seem to be on the edge of an unbounded light . . .

ALLADINE.

Come! come! I have borne without a word, but I can bear no more . . .

PALOMIDES (groping forward).

You are there? I thought you so far away! . . . My tears deceived me. I am here, and I see you. Oh, your hands are wounded! They have bled upon your gown, and the knots have entered into the flesh. I have no longer any weapons. They have taken away my poniard. I will tear them off. Wait! wait! I have the knots.

ALLADINE.

Take off the bandage first that makes me blind . . .

PALOMIDES.

I cannot . . . I do not see . . . It seems to be surrounded by a net of golden threads . . .

ALLADINE.

My hands, then, my hands!

PALOMIDES.

They have taken silken cords ... Wait, the knots come undone. The cord has thirty turns ... There, there!—Oh, your hands are all blood! ... You would say they were dead ...

ALLADINE.

No, no! ... They are alive! they are alive! See! ...
[*With her hands hardly yet unbound, she clasps Palomides about the neck and kisses him passionately.*]

PALOMIDES.

Alladine!

ALLADINE.

Palomides!

PALOMIDES.

Alladine, Alladine! ...

ALLADINE.

I am happy! ... I have waited a long while! ...

PALOMIDES.

I was afraid to come ...

ALLADINE.

I am happy ... and I would that I could see thee ...

PALOMIDES.

They have tied down the bandage like a casque . . .—Do not turn round; I have found the golden threads . . .

ALLADINE.

Yes, yes, I will turn round . . .
[She turns about, to kiss him again.

PALOMIDES.

Have a care. Do not stir. I am afraid of wounding thee . . .

ALLADINE.

Tear it away! Fear nothing. I can bear no more! . . .

PALOMIDES.

I would see thee too . . .

ALLADINE.

Tear it away! Tear it away! I am no longer within reach of woe! . . . Tear it away! . . . Thou dost not know that one could wish to die . . . Where are we?

PALOMIDES.

Thou'lt see, thou'lt see . . . It is innumerable crypts . . . great blue halls, gleaming pillars, and deep vaults . . .

ALLADINE.

Why dost thou answer when I question thee?

PALOMIDES.

What matter where we be, if we be but together? . . .

ALLADINE.

Thou lovest me less already?

PALOMIDES.

Why, what ails thee?

ALLADINE.

I know well where I am when I am on thy heart . . . Oh, tear the bandage off! . . . I would not enter blind into thy soul . . . What doest thou, Palomides? Thou dost not laugh when I laugh. Thou dost not weep when I weep. Thou dost not clap thy hands when I clap mine; and thou tremblest not when I speak trembling to the bottom of my soul . . . The band! The band! . . . I will see! . . . There, there, above my hair! . . . [*She tears away the bandage.*] Oh! . . .

PALOMIDES.

Seest thou?

ALLADINE.

Yes . . . I see thee only . . .

PALOMIDES.

What is it, Alladine? Thou kissest me as if thou wert already sad . . .

ALLADINE.

Where are we?

PALOMIDES.

Why dost thou ask so sadly?

ALLADINE.

No, I am not sad; but my eyes will hardly open . . .

PALOMIDES.

One would say your joy had fallen on my lips like a child at the threshold of the house . . . Do not turn away . . . I fear lest you should flee, and I fear lest I dream . . .

ALLADINE.

Where are we?

PALOMIDES.

We are in crypts that I have never seen . . . Doth it not seem to thee the light increases? When I unclosed my eyes, I could distinguish nothing; now little by little it is all revealed. I have been often told of wondrous caverns whereon the halls of Ablamore were built. It must be these. No one descends here ever; and the king only has the keys. I knew the sea flooded the lowest vaults; and it is probably the reflex of the sea which thus illumines us . . . They thought to bury us in night. They came down here with torches and flambeaus and saw the darkness only, while the light came out to meet us, seeing we had none . . . It brightens without ceasing . . . I am sure the dawn pierces the ocean and sends down to us through all its greening waves the purest of its child-soul . . .

ALLADINE.

How long have we been here?

PALOMIDES.

I have no idea . . . I made no effort till I heard thee speak . . .

ALLADINE.

I do not know how this took place. I was asleep in the room where thou didst find me; and when I waked, my eyes were bound across, and both my hands were pinioned in my girdle . . .

PALOMIDES.

I too was sleeping. I heard nothing, and I had a band across my eyes ere I could open them. I struggled in the darkness; but they were stronger than I . . . I must have passed under deep vaults, for I felt the cold fall on my shoulders; and I went down so far I could not count the steps . . . Did no one speak to thee?

ALLADINE.

No; no one spoke. I heard some one weeping as he walked; and then I fainted . . .

PALOMIDES (kissing her).

Alladine!

ALLADINE.

How gravely thou dost kiss me! . . .

PALOMIDES.

Close not thine eyes when I do kiss thee so . . . I would see the kisses trembling in thy heart, and all the dew that rises in thy soul . . . We shall not find such kisses any more . . .

ALLADINE.

Always, always!

PALOMIDES.

No, no; there is no kissing twice upon the heart of death . . . How fair thou art so! . . . It is the first time I have seen thee near . . . It is strange, we think that we have seen each other because we have gone by two steps apart; but everything changes the moment the lips touch . . . There, thou must be let to have thy will . . . I stretch my arms wide to admire thee, as if thou wert no longer mine; and then

I draw them nearer till I touch thy kisses and perceive only eternal bliss . . . There needed us this supernatural light! . . . [*He kisses her again.*] Ah! What hast thou done? Take care! we are upon a crest of rock that overhangs the water that gives us light. Do not step back. It was time . . . Do not turn too abruptly. I was dazzled . . .

ALLADINE.

[*Turning and looking at the blue water that illuminates them.*] Oh! . . .

PALOMIDES.

It is as if the sky had flowed hither . . .

ALLADINE.

It is full of moveless flowers . . .

PALOMIDES.

It is full of moveless flowers and strange . . . Hast thou seen the largest there that blooms beneath the others? It seems to live a cadenced life . . . And the water . . . Is it water? . . . It seems more beautiful, more pure, more blue than all the water in the world . . .

ALLADINE.

I dare not look upon it longer . . .

PALOMIDES.

See how about us all is luminous . . . The light dares hesitate no longer, and we kiss each other in the vestibules of heaven . . . Seest thou the precious stones that gem the vaults, drunken with life, that seem to smile on us; and the thousands and thousands of glowing blue roses that climb along the pillars? . . .

144

ALLADINE.

Oh! . . . I heard! . . .

PALOMIDES.

What?

ALLADINE.

Some one striking the rocks . . .

PALOMIDES.

No, no; it is the golden gates of a new Paradise, that open in our souls and sing upon their hinges! . . .

ALLADINE.

Listen . . . again, again! . . .

PALOMIDES (with voice suddenly changed).

Yes; it is there . . . It is at the bottom of the bluest vaults . . .

ALLADINE.

They are coming to . . .

PALOMIDES.

I hear the sound of iron on the rock . . . They have walled up the door or cannot open it . . . It is the picks grating against the stone . . . His soul has told him we were happy . . .
[A silence; then a stone is detached at the very end of the vault, and a ray of daylight breaks into the cavern.]

ALLADINE.

Oh! . . .

PALOMIDES.

It is another light . . .

[*Motionless and anxious, they watch other stones detach themselves slowly in an insufferable light, and fall one by one; while the light, entering in more and more resistless floods, reveals to them little by little the gloom of the cavern they had thought marvellous. The miraculous lake becomes wan and sinister; the precious stones about them are extinguished, and the glowing roses appear as the stains and rotten rubbish that they are. At last, the whole side of rock falls abruptly into the crypt. The sunlight enters, dazzling. Calls and songs are heard without. Alladine and Palomides recoil.*]

PALOMIDES.

Where are we?

ALLADINE (embracing him).

I love thee still, Palomides . . .

PALOMIDES.

I love thee too, my Alladine . . .

ALLADINE.

They come . . .

PALOMIDES.

[*Looking behind him as they still recoil.*] Have a care . . .

ALLADINE.

No, no; have no more care . . .

PALOMIDES (looking at her).

Alladine?

ALLADINE.

Yes . . .

[*They still recoil before the invasion of light or peril, until they lose their footing; and they fall and disappear behind the rock that overhangs the underground and now gloomy water.—A silence. Astolaine and the sisters of Palomides enter the crypt.*]

ASTOLAINE.

Where are they?

ONE OF THE SISTERS OF PALOMIDES.

Palomides! . . .

ASTOLAINE.

Alladine! Alladine! . . .

ANOTHER SISTER.

Palomides! . . . It is we! . . .

THIRD SISTER.

Fear nothing; we are alone! . . .

ASTOLAINE.

Come! come! we have come to rescue you! . . .

FOURTH SISTER.

Ablamore has fled . . .

FIFTH SISTER.

He is no longer in the palace . . .

SIXTH SISTER.
They do not answer . . .

ASTOLAINE.
I heard the water stirred! . . . This way, this way!

[They run to the rock that overlooks the underground.]

ONE OF THE SISTERS.
They are there! . . .

ANOTHER SISTER.
Yes, yes; at the very bottom of the black water . . . They embrace.

THIRD SISTER.
They are dead.

FOURTH SISTER.
No, no; they are alive! they are alive! . . . See . . .

THE OTHER SISTERS.
Help! help! . . . Call! . . .

ASTOLAINE.
They make no effort to save themselves! . . .

ACT FIFTH.

[A corridor, so long that its furthest arches seem to lose themselves in a kind of indoor horizon. The sisters of Palomides wait before one of the innumerable closed doors that open into this corridor. They seem to be guarding it. A little further down, on the opposite side, Astolaine and the Physician converse before another door, also closed.]

ASTOLAINE.

[To the Physician.] Nothing has ever happened until now in this palace, where all things have seemed to be asleep since my sisters died; and my poor old father, pursued by a strange restlessness, has fretted without reason at this calm, which seems, for all that, the least dangerous form of happiness. Some time ago,—his reason beginning to totter even then,—he went up to the top of a high tower; and as he stretched his arms out timidly toward the forests and toward the sea, he said to me—smiling a little fearfully at his words, as if to disarm my incredulous smile—that he called about us events which had long been hidden beneath the horizon. They have come, alas! sooner and more in number than he expected, and a few days have sufficed for them to reign in his stead. He has been their first victim. He fled to the meadows, singing, all in tears, the evening when he had little Alladine and luckless Palomides taken down into the crypts. He has not since been seen. I have had search made everywhere throughout the country and even on the sea. He has not been found. At least, I had hoped to save those he made suffer unwittingly, for he has always been the tenderest of men and the best of fathers; but there, too, I think I came too late. I do not know what happened. They have not spoken yet. They doubtless must have thought, hearing the sound of the iron and seeing all at once the light again, that my father had regretted the kind of surcease he had granted them, and that some

one came to bring them death. Or else they slipped as they drew back, upon the rock that overhangs the lake; and so must have fallen through heedlessness. But the water is not deep in that spot, and we succeeded in saving them without difficulty. To-day it is you alone who can do the rest.

[THE SISTERS OF PALOMIDES have drawn nearer.

THE PHYSICIAN.

They are both ailing with the same disease, and it is a disease I do not know.—But I have little hope left. They were seized perhaps with the cold of the underground waters; or else those waters may be poisonous. The decomposed body of Alladine's lamb was found there.—I will come back to-night.—Meanwhile they must have silence . . . The level of life is very low in their hearts . . . Do not go into their rooms and do not speak to them, for the least word, in the state they are in, might cause their death . . . They must succeed in forgetting one another. [Exit.

ONE OF THE SISTERS OF PALOMIDES.

I see that he will die.

ASTOLAINE.

No, no . . . Do not weep; . . . one does not die so, at his age . . .

ANOTHER SISTER.

But why is your father angry without reason at my poor brother?

THIRD SISTER.

I think your father loved Alladine.

ASTOLAINE.

Do not speak so of it . . . He thought I suffered. He thought to have done good, and he did evil unwittingly . . . That often happens to us . . . It is my fault, perhaps . . . I recall it to-day . . . One night I was asleep. I was weeping in a dream . . . We have little courage when we dream. I waked . . . He was beside my bed, looking at me . . . Perhaps he was deceived . . .

FOURTH SISTER *(running)*.

Alladine has stirred a little in her room . . .

ASTOLAINE.

Go to the door . . . listen . . . Perhaps it was the nurse rising . . .

FIFTH SISTER *(listening at the door)*.

No, no; I hear the nurse walking . . . There is another noise.

SIXTH SISTER *(also running)*.

I think Palomides has moved too; I hear the murmur of a voice seeking . . .

THE VOICE OF ALLADINE.

[Very feebly, within the room.] Palomides! . . .

ONE OF THE SISTERS.

She is calling him! . . .

ASTOLAINE.

Let us be careful! . . . Go, go in front of the door, that Palomides may not hear . . .

THE VOICE OF ALLADINE.

Palomides!

ASTOLAINE.

My God! My God! Silence that voice! . . . Palomides will die of it if he hear it! . . .

THE VOICE OF PALOMIDES.

[*Very feebly, within the other room.*] Alladine! . . .

ONE OF THE SISTERS.

He answers! . . .

ASTOLAINE.

Three among you remain here, . . . and we will go to the other door. Come, come quickly. We will surround them. We will try to defend them . . . Lie back against the doors . . . Perhaps they will hear no longer . . .

ONE OF THE SISTERS.

I shall go into Alladine's room . . .

SECOND SISTER.

Yes, yes; prevent her from crying out again.

THIRD SISTER.

She is already cause of all this evil . . .

ASTOLAINE.

Do not go in, or I go in to Palomides . . . She also had a right to life; and she has done nought but to live . . . But that we cannot stifle in their passage their deadly words! . . . We are without help, my poor sisters, my poor sisters, and hands cannot stop souls! . . .

THE VOICE OF ALLADINE.
Palomides, is it thou?

THE VOICE OF PALOMIDES.
Where art thou, Alladine?

THE VOICE OF ALLADINE.
Is it thou whom I hear far from me making moan?

THE VOICE OF PALOMIDES.
Is it thou whom I hear calling, and see thee not?

THE VOICE OF ALLADINE.
One would believe thy voice had lost the last of hope . . .

THE VOICE OF PALOMIDES.
One would believe that thine had crossed the winds of death . . .

THE VOICE OF ALLADINE.
It goes hard with thy voice to pierce into my room . . .

THE VOICE OF PALOMIDES.
And I no longer hear thy voice as of old time.

THE VOICE OF ALLADINE.
I have been woe for thee! . . .

THE VOICE OF PALOMIDES.
They have divided us, but I do love thee ever . . .

THE VOICE OF ALLADINE.

I have been woe for thee . . . Art then still suffering?

THE VOICE OF PALOMIDES.

No; I no longer suffer, but I =fain= would see thee . . .

THE VOICE OF ALLADINE.

We shall not see each other more; the doors are shut . . .

THE VOICE OF PALOMIDES.

Thy voice would make one say thou lovedst me no more . . .

THE VOICE OF ALLADINE.

Yes, yes; I love thee still, but it is mournful now . . .

THE VOICE OF PALOMIDES.

Whither is thy face turned? I hardly understand thee . . .

THE VOICE OF ALLADINE.

We seem to be an hundred leagues from one another . . .

THE VOICE OF PALOMIDES.

I try to rise in vain; my spirit is too heavy . . .

THE VOICE OF ALLADINE.

I too would come,—I too—but still my head falls back . . .

THE VOICE OF PALOMIDES.

Thou seemest almost to speak in tears despite thyself . . .

THE VOICE OF ALLADINE.

No; I wept long ago; it is no longer tears . . .

THE VOICE OF PALOMIDES.

There's something in thy thoughts thou dost not tell me of . . .

THE VOICE OF ALLADINE.

They were not precious stones . . .

THE VOICE OF PALOMIDES.

And the flowers were not real . . .

ONE OF THE SISTERS OF PALOMIDES.

They rave . . .

ASTOLAINE.

No, no; they know what they are saying . . .

THE VOICE OF ALLADINE.

It was the light that had no pity on us . . .

THE VOICE OF PALOMIDES.

Where goest thou, Alladine? Thou'rt being borne away . . .

THE VOICE OF ALLADINE.

I have no more regret to lose the light o' the sun . . .

THE VOICE OF PALOMIDES.

Yes, yes; we shall behold the sweet green things again! . . .

THE VOICE OF ALLADINE.

I have lost desire to live . . .

[*A silence; then more and more faintly:*]

THE VOICE OF PALOMIDES.

Alladine! . . .

THE VOICE OF ALLADINE.

Palomides! . . .

THE VOICE OF PALOMIDES.

Alla . . . dine! . . .

[A silence.—Astolaine and the sisters of Palomides listen, in anguish. Then the nurse opens, from the inside, the door of Palomides' room, appears on the sill, makes a sign, and all enter the room. The door closes behind them. A new silence. A little afterwards, the door of Alladine's room opens in its turn; the other nurse comes out in like manner, looks about in the corridor, and, seeing no one, re-enters the room, leaving the door wide open.]

[CURTAIN.]

HOME.

To Mademoiselle Sara de Swart.

PERSONS.

IN THE GARDEN.

THE OLD MAN.
THE STRANGER.
MARTHA   } *granddaughters of the old man.*
AND MARY,   }
A PEASANT. THE CROWD.

IN THE HOUSE

THE FATHER,   }
THE MOTHER,   } *Silent characters.*
THE TWO DAUGHTERS,   }
THE CHILD,   }

[An old garden, planted with willows. At the back, a house in which three windows on the ground-floor are lighted. A family, sitting up under the lamp, is seen rather distinctly. The father is seated by the fireside. The mother, one elbow on the table, is staring into space. Two young girls, clad in white, embroider, dream, and smile in the quiet of the room. A child lies asleep with his head under the mother's left arm. Whenever one of them rises, walks, or makes a gesture, his movements seem to be grave, slow, rare, and, as it were, spiritualized by the distance, the light, and the vague veil of the windows. The old man and the stranger enter the garden cautiously.]

THE OLD MAN.

We are in the part of the garden behind the house. They never come here. The doors are on the other side.—They are closed, and the shutters are up. But there are no shutters on this side, and I saw a light . . . Yes; they are sitting up still under the lamp. It is fortunate they have not heard us; the mother or the young girls would have come out, perhaps, and then what should we have done? . . .

THE STRANGER.

What are we going to do?

THE OLD MAN.

I should like to see, first, if they are all in the room. Yes, I see the father sitting in the chimney-corner. He waits, with his hands on his knees; . . . the mother is resting her elbow on the table.

THE STRANGER.

She is looking at us . . .

THE OLD MAN.

No; she doesn't know where she is looking: her eyes do not wink. She cannot see us; we are in the shade of great trees. But do not go any nearer . . . The two sisters of the dead girl are in the room too. They are embroidering slowly; and the little child is asleep. It is nine by the clock in the corner . . . They suspect nothing, and they do not speak.

THE STRANGER.

If one could draw the father's attention, and make him some sign? He has turned his head this way. Would you like me to knock at one of the windows? One of them ought to be told before the others . . .

THE OLD MAN.

I don't know which one to choose . . . We must take great precautions . . . The father is old and ailing . . . So is the mother; and the sisters are too young . . . And they all loved her with such love as will never be again . . . I never saw a happier household . . . No, no, do not go near the window; that would be worse than anything else . . . It is better to announce it as simply as possible,—as if it were an ordinary event,—and not to look too sad; for otherwise their grief will wish to be greater than yours and will know of nothing more that it can do . . . Let us go on the other side of the garden. We will knock at the door and go in as if nothing had happened. I will go in first: they will not be surprised to see me; I come sometimes in the evening, to bring them flowers or fruit, and pass a few hours with them.

THE STRANGER.

Why must I go with you? Go alone; I will wait till I am called . . . They have never seen me . . . I am only a passer-by; I am a stranger . . .

THE OLD MAN.

It is better not to be alone. A sorrow that one does not bring alone is not so unmixed nor so heavy . . . I was thinking of that as we were coming here . . . If I go in alone, I shall have to be speaking from the first minute; in a few words they will know everything, and I shall have nothing more to say; and I am afraid of the silence following the last words that announce a woe . . . It is then the heart is rent . . . If we go in together, I shall tell them, for example, after going a long way about, "She was found so . . . She was floating in the river, and her hands were clasped." . . .

THE STRANGER.

Her hands were not clasped; her arms were hanging down along her body.

THE OLD MAN.

You see, one speaks in spite of oneself . . . And the sorrow is lost in the details; . . . but otherwise, if I go in alone, at the first words, knowing them as I do, it would be dreadful, and God knows what might happen . . . But if we speak in turn, they will listen to us and not think to look the ill news in the face . . . Do not forget the mother will be there, and that her life hangs by a thread . . . It is good that the first wave break on some unnecessary words . . . There should be a little talking around the unhappy, and they should have people about them . . . The most indifferent bear unwittingly a part of the grief . . . So, without noise or effort, it divides, like air or light . . .

THE STRANGER.

Your clothes are wet through; they are dripping on the flagstones.

THE OLD MAN.

It is only the bottom of my cloak that dipped in the water.—You seem to be cold. Your chest is covered with earth . . . I did not notice it on the road on account of the darkness . . .

THE STRANGER.

I went into the water up to my waist.

THE OLD MAN.

Was it long after you found her when I came?

THE STRANGER.

A few minutes, barely. I was going toward the village; it was already late, and the bank was getting dark. I was walking with my eyes fixed on the river because it was lighter than the road, when I saw something strange a step or two from a clump of reeds . . . I drew near and made out her hair, which had risen almost in a circle above her head, and whirled round, so, in the current.

[In the room, the two young girls turn their heads toward the window.]

THE OLD MAN.

Did you see the two sisters' hair quiver on their shoulders?

THE STRANGER.

They turned their heads this way . . . They simply turned their heads. Perhaps I spoke too loud. *[The two young girls resume their former position.]* But they are already looking no longer . . . I went into the water up to my waist and I was able to take her by the hand and pull her without effort to the shore . . . She was as beautiful as her sisters are.

THE OLD MAN.

She was perhaps more beautiful . . . I do not know why I have lost all courage . . .

THE STRANGER.

What courage are you talking of? We have done all man could do . . . She was dead more than an hour ago . . .

THE OLD MAN.

She was alive this morning! . . . I met her coming out of church . . . She told me she was going away; she was going to see her grandmother on the other side of the river where you found her . . . She did not know when I should see her again . . . She must have been on the point of asking me something; then she dared not and left me abruptly. But I think of it now . . . And I saw nothing! . . . She smiled as they smile who choose to be silent, or who are afraid they will not be understood . . . She seemed hardly to hope . . . Her eyes were not clear and hardly looked at me . . .

THE STRANGER.

Some peasants told me they had seen her wandering on the river-bank until nightfall . . . They thought she was looking for flowers . . . It may be that her death . . .

THE OLD MAN.

We cannot tell . . . What is there we can tell? . . . She was perhaps of those who do not wish to speak, and every one of us bears in himself more than one reason for no longer living . . . We cannot see in the soul as we see in that room. They are all like that . . . They only say trite things; and no one suspects aught . . . You live for months by some one who is no longer of this world and whose soul can bend no longer; you answer without thinking; and you see what happens . . . They look like motionless dolls, and, oh, the events that take place in their souls! . . . They do not know themselves what they are . . . She would have lived as the rest live . . . She would have said up to her death: "Monsieur, Madame, we shall have rain this morning," or else, "We are going to breakfast; we shall be thirteen at table," or else: "The fruits are not yet ripe." They speak with a smile of the flowers that have fallen, and weep in the dark . . . An angel even would not see what should be seen; and man only understands when it is too late . . . Yesterday evening she was there, under the lamp like her sisters, and you would not see them as they should be seen, if this had not occurred . . . I seem to see her now for the first time . . . Something must be added to common life before we can understand it . . . They are beside you day and night, and you perceive them only at the moment when they depart forever . . . And yet the strange little soul she must have had; the poor, naïve, exhaustless little soul she had, my son, if she said what she must have said, if she did what she mast have done! . . .

THE STRANGER.

Just now they are smiling in silence in the room . . .

THE OLD MAN.

They are at peace . . . They did not expect her to-night . . .

THE STRANGER.

They smile without stirring; . . . and see, the father is putting his finger on his lips . . .

THE OLD MAN.

He is calling attention to the child asleep on its mother's heart . . .

THE STRANGER.

She dares not raise her eyes lest she disturb its sleep . . .

THE OLD MAN.

They are no longer working . . . A great silence reigns . . .

THE STRANGER.

They have let fell the skein of white silk . . .

THE OLD MAN.

They are watching the child . . .

THE STRANGER.

They do not know that others are watching them . . .

THE OLD MAN.

   We are watched too . . .

THE STRANGER.

   They have lifted their eyes . . .

THE OLD MAN.

   And yet they can see nothing . . .

THE STRANGER.

   They seem happy; and yet nobody knows what may be—. . .

THE OLD MAN.

   They think themselves in safety . . . They have shut the doors; and
   the windows have iron bars . . . They have mended the walls of the
   old house; they have put bolts upon the oaken doors . . . They have
   foreseen all that could be foreseen . . .

THE STRANGER.

   We must end by telling them . . . Some one might come and let them
   know abruptly . . . There was a crowd of peasants in the meadow
   where the dead girl was found . . . If one of them knocked at the
   door . . .

THE OLD MAN.

   Martha and Mary are beside the poor dead child. The peasants were
   to make a litter of leaves; and I told the elder to come warn us in all
   haste, the moment they began their march. Let us wait till she comes;
   she will go in with me . . . We should not have looked on them so . . .
   I thought it would be only to knock upon the door; to go in simply,
   find a phrase or two, and tell . . . But I have seen them live too long
   under their lamp . . .

Enter MARY.

MARY.

They are coming, grandfather.

THE OLD MAN.

Is It you?—Where are they?

MARY.

They are at the foot of the last hills.

THE OLD MAN.

They will come in silence?

MARY.

I told them to pray in a low voice. Martha is with them . . .

THE OLD MAN.

Are they many?

MARY.

The whole village is about the bearers. They had brought lights. I told them to put them out . . .

THE OLD MAN.

Which way are they coming?

MARY.

They are coming by the footpaths. They are walking slowly . . .

THE OLD MAN.

It is time . . .

MARY.

You have told them, grandfather?

THE OLD MAN.

You see plainly we have told them nothing . . . They are waiting still under the lamp . . . Look, my child, look! You will see something of life . . .

MARY.

Oh, how at peace they seem! . . . You would say I saw them in a dream . . .

THE STRANGER.

Take care, I saw both sisters give a start . . .

THE OLD MAN.

They are getting up . . .

THE STRANGER.

I think they are coming to the windows . . .

[At this moment, one of the two sisters of whom they speak draws near the first window, the other near the third, and, pressing their hands at the same time against the panes, look a long while into the darkness.]

THE OLD MAN.

No one comes to the window in the middle . . .

MARY.

They are looking . . . They are listening . . .

THE OLD MAN.

The elder smiles at what she does not see.

THE STRANGER.

And the other has eyes full of fearfulness . . .

THE OLD MAN.

Take care; we do not know how far the soul extends about men . . .

[*A long silence*, MARY *cowers against the old man's breast and kisses him.*]

MARY.

Grandfather! . . .

THE OLD MAN.

Do not weep, my child . . . We shall have our turn . . .

[*A silence.*

THE STRANGER.

They are looking a long while . . .

THE OLD MAN.

They might look a hundred thousand years and not perceive anything, the poor little sisters . . . The night is too dark . . . They are looking this way; and it is from that way the misfortune is coming . . .

THE STRANGER.

It is fortunate they look this way . . . I do not know what that is coming toward us, over by the meadows.

MARY.

I think it is the crowd . . . They are so far away you can hardly make them out . . .

THE STRANGER.

They follow the undulations of the path . . . Now they appear again on a hillside in the moonlight . . .

MARY.

Oh, how many they seem! . . . They had already run up from the suburbs of the city when I came . . . They are going a long way around . . .

THE OLD MAN.

They will come in spite of all; I see them too . . . They are on the march across the meadow lands . . . They seem so small you hardly make them out among the grasses . . . They look like children playing in the moonlight; and if the girls should see them, they would not understand . . . In vain they turn their backs; those yonder draw near with every step they take, and the sorrow has been growing these two hours already. They cannot hinder it from growing; and they that bear it there no longer can arrest it . . . It is their master too, and they must serve it . . . It has its end and follows its own road . . . It is unwearying and has but one idea . . . Needs must they lend their strength. They are sad, but they come . . . They have pity, but they must go forward . . .

MARY.

The elder smiles no longer, grandfather . . .

THE STRANGER.

They leave the windows . . .

MARY.

They kiss their mother . . .

THE STRANGER.

The elder has caressed the curls of the child without waking him . . .

MARY.

Oh! the father wants to be kissed too . . .

THE STRANGER.

And now silence . . .

MARY.

They come back beside the mother . . .

THE STRANGER.

And the father follows the great pendulum of the clock with his eyes . . .

MARY.

You would say they were praying without knowing what they did . . .

THE STRANGER.

You would say that they were listening to their souls . . .

[A silence.

MARY.

Grandfather, don't tell them to-night! . . .

THE OLD MAN.

You see, you too lose courage . . . I knew well that we must not look. I am nearly eighty-three years old, and this is the first time the sight of life has struck me. I do not know why everything they do seems so strange and grave to me . . . They wait for night quite simply, under their lamp, as we might have been waiting under ours; and yet I seem to see them from the height of another world, because I know a little truth which they do not know yet . . . Is it that, my children? Tell me, then, why you are pale, too? Is there something else, perhaps, that cannot be told and causes us to weep? I did not know there was anything so sad in life, nor that it frightened those who looked upon it . . . And nothing can have occurred that I should be afraid to see them so at peace . . . They have too much confidence in this world . . . There they are, separated from the enemy by a poor window . . . They think nothing will happen because they have shut the door, and do not know that something is always happening in our souls, and that the world does not end at the doors of our houses . . . They are so sure of their little life and do not suspect how many others know more of it than they; and that I, poor old man,—I hold here, two steps from their door, all their little happiness, like a sick bird, in my old hands I do not dare to open . . .

MARY.

Have pity, grandfather . . .

THE OLD MAN.

We have pity on them, my child, but no one has pity on us . . .

MARY.

Tell them to-morrow, grandfather; tell them when it is light . . . They will not be so sorrowful . . .

174

THE OLD MAN.

Perhaps you are right, my child . . . It would be better to leave all this in the night. And the light is sweet to sorrow . . . But what would they say to us to-morrow? Misfortune renders jealous; they whom it strikes, wish to be told before strangers; they do not like to have it left in the hands of those they do not know . . . We should look as if we had stolen something . . .

THE STRANGER.

There is no more time, besides; I hear the murmur of prayers already . . .

MARY.

There they are . . . They are passing behind the hedges . . .

Enter MARTHA.

MARTHA.

Here I am. I have brought them this far. I have told them to wait on the road. [*Cries of children heard.*] Ah! the children are crying again . . . I forbade their coming . . . But they wanted to see too, and the mothers would not obey . . . I will go tell them . . . No; they are silent.—Is everything ready?—I have brought the little ring that was found on her . . . I have some fruit, too, for the child . . . I laid her out myself on the litter. She looks as if she were asleep . . . I had a good deal of trouble; her hair would not obey . . . I had some marguerites plucked . . . It is sad, there were no other flowers . . . What are you doing here? Why are you not by them? . . . [*She looks at the windows.*] They do not weep? . . . They . . . you have not told them?

THE OLD MAN.

Martha, Martha, there is too much life in your soul; you cannot understand . . .

MARTHA.

Why should I not understand? . . . [*After a silence and in a tone of very grave reproach.*] You cannot have done that, grandfather . . .

THE OLD MAN.

Martha, you do not know . . .

MARTHA.

I will tell them.

THE OLD MAN.

Stay here, my child, and look at them a moment.

MARTHA.

Oh, how unhappy they are! . . . They can wait no longer.

THE OLD MAN.

Why?

MARTHA.

I do not know; . . . it is no longer possible! . . .

THE OLD MAN.

Come here, my child . . .

MARTHA.

How patient they are!

THE OLD MAN.

Come here, my child . . .

MARTHA.

[Turning.] Where are you, grandfather? I am so unhappy I cannot see you any more . . . I do not know what to do myself any more . . .

THE OLD MAN.

Do not look at them any more; till they know all . . .

MARTHA.

I will go in with you . . .

THE OLD MAN.

No, Martha, stay here . . . Sit beside your sister, on this old stone bench, against the wall of the house, and do not look . . . You are too young; you never could forget . . . You cannot know what a face is like at the moment when death passes before its eyes . . . There will be cries, perhaps . . . Do not turn round . . . Perhaps there will be nothing . . . Above all, do not turn if you hear nothing . . . One does not know the course of grief beforehand . . . A few little deep-rooted sobs, and that is all, usually . . . I do not know myself what I may do when I shall hear them . . . That belongs no longer to this life . . . Kiss me, my child, before I go away . . .

[The murmur of prayers has gradually drawn nearer. Part of the crowd invades the garden. Dull steps heard, running, and low voices speaking.]

THE STRANGER *(to the crowd)*.

Stay here; . . . do not go near the windows . . . Where is she? . . .

A PEASANT.
  Who?

THE STRANGER.
  The rest . . . the bearers? . . .

THE PEASANT.
  They are coming by the walk that leads to the door.

[The old man goes away. Martha and Mary are seated on the bench, with their backs turned to the windows. Murmurs in the crowd.]

THE STRANGER.
  S—t! . . . Do not speak.

[The elder of the two sisters rises and goes to bolt the door . . .]

MARTHA.
  She opens it?

THE STRANGER.
  On the contrary, she is shutting it.

[A silence.

MARTHA.
  Grandfather has not entered?

THE STRANGER.
  No . . . She returns and sits down by her mother . . . The others do not stir, and the child sleeps all the time . . .

[A silence.

MARTHA.

Sister, give me your hands . . .

MARY.

Martha! . . .
[They embrace and give each other a kiss.

THE STRANGER.

He must have knocked . . . They have all raised their heads at the same time; . . . they look at each other . . .

MARTHA.

Oh! oh! my poor little sister! . . . I shall cry too! . . .

[She stifles her sobs on her sister's shoulder.

THE STRANGER.

He must be knocking again . . . The father looks at the clock. He rises.

MARTHA.

Sister, sister, I want to go in too . . . They cannot be alone any longer . . .

MARY.

Martha! Martha! . . .

[She holds her back.

THE STRANGER.

The father is at the door . . . He draws the bolts . . . He opens the
door prudently . . .

MARTHA.

Oh! . . . you do not see the . . .

THE STRANGER.

What?

MARTHA.

Those who bear . . .

THE STRANGER.

He hardly opens it . . . I can only see a corner of the lawn; and the
fountain . . . He does not let go the door; . . . he steps back . . . He
looks as if he were saying: "Ah, it's you!" . . . He raises his arms . . .
He shuts the door again carefully . . . Your grandfather has come into
the room . . .

*[The crowd has drawn nearer the windows. Martha and Mary half rise at first,
then draw near also, clasping each other tightly. The old man is seen advancing
into the room. The two sisters of the dead girl rise; the mother rises as well, after
laying the child carefully in the armchair she has just abandoned; in such a way
that from without the little one may be seen asleep, with his head hanging a little
to one side, in the centre of the room. The mother advances to meet the old man
and extends her hand to him, but draws it back before he has had time to take
it. One of the young girls offers to take off the visitor's cloak and the other brings
forward a chair for him; but the old man makes a slight gesture of refusal. The
father smiles with a surprised look. The old man looks toward the windows.]*

THE STRANGER.

He dares not tell them . . . He has looked at us . . .

[Rumors in the crowd.

THE STRANGER.

S . . . t! . . .

[The old man, seeing their faces at the windows, has quickly turned his eyes away. As one of the young girls continues to offer him the same armchair, he ends by sitting down and passes his right hand across his forehead several times.]

THE STRANGER.

He sits down . . .

[The other people in the room sit down also, while the father talks volubly. At last the old man opens his mouth, and the tone of his voice seems to attract attention. But the father interrupts him. The old man begins to speak again, and little by little the others become motionless. All at once, the mother starts and rises.]

MARTHA.

Oh! the mother is going to understand! . . .

[She turns away and hides her face in her hands. New murmurs in the crowd. They elbow each other. Children cry to be lifted up, so that they may see too. Most of the mothers obey.]

THE STRANGER.

S . . . t! . . . He has not told them yet . . .
[The mother is seen to question the old man in anguish. He says a few words more; then abruptly all the rest rise too and seem to question him. He makes a slow sign of affirmation with his head.]

THE STRANGER.

He has told them . . . He has told them all at once! . . .

VOICES IN THE CROWD.

He has told them! . . . He has told them! . . .

THE STRANGER.

You hear nothing . . .

[*The old man rises too, and, without turning, points with his finger to the door behind him. The mother, the father, and the two young girls throw themselves on this door, which the father cannot at once succeed in opening. The old man tries to prevent the mother from going out.*]

VOICES IN THE CROWD.

They are going out! They are going out! . . .

[*Jostling in the garden. All rush to the other side of the house and disappear, with the exception of the stranger, who remains at the windows. In the room, both sides of the folding-door at last open; all go out at the same time. Beyond can be seen a starry sky, the lawn and the fountain in the moonlight, while in the middle of the abandoned room the child continues to sleep peacefully in the armchair.—Silence.*]

THE STRANGER.

The child has not waked! . . .

[*He goes out also.*

[CURTAIN.]

Lightning Source UK Ltd.
Milton Keynes UK
UKOW04f0609090517

300805UK00011B/844/P